THE
WEB WIZARD'S
GUIDE TO
FLASH

THE
WEB WIZARD'S
GUIDE TO
FLASH

MICHAEL R. KAY

Addison
Wesley

Boston San Francisco New York
London Toronto Sydney Tokyo Singapore Madrid
Mexico City Munich Paris Cape Town Hong Kong Montreal

Executive Editor: *Susan Hartman Sullivan*
Assistant Editor: *Galia Shokry*
Associate Managing Editor: *Pat Mahtani*
Executive Marketing Manager: *Michael Hirsch*
Production Supervision: *Kathy Smith*
Cover and Interior Designer: *Leslie Haimes*
Composition: *Gillian Hall, The Aardvark Group*
Copyeditor: *Kathy Smith*
Proofreader: *Holly McLean-Aldis*
Design Manager: *Gina Hagen Kolenda*
Prepress and Manufacturing: *Caroline Fell*

Access the latest information about Addison-Wesley titles from our World Wide Web site: *http://www.aw.com/cs*

Macromedia is a registered trademark, and Macromedia, Flash, and Dreamweaver are trademarks of Macromedia.

Throughout this book, trademarked names are used. Rather than put a trademark symbol in each occurrence of a trademarked name, we state we are using the names only in an editorial fashion and to the benefit of the trademark owner and with no intention of infringement on the trademark.

The programs and applications presented in this book have been included for their instructional value. They have been tested with care, but are not guaranteed for any particular purpose. The publisher does not offer any warranties or representations, nor does it accept any liabilities with respect to the programs or applications.

Library of Congress Cataloging-in-Publication Data
Kay, Michael (Michael R.), 1962–
   The Web Wizard's guide to Flash / Michael Kay.
      p. cm.
   ISBN 0-201-76434-2
   1. Computer animation. 2. Flash (Computer file) 3. Web sites--Design. I. Title.

TR897.7 .K39 2002
006.6'96--dc21   2002066949

12345678910—QWT—040302

TABLE OF CONTENTS

PREFACE

About Addison-Wesley's Web Wizard Series

The beauty of the Web is that, with a little effort, anyone can harness its power to create sophisticated Web sites. Addison-Wesley's Web Wizard Series helps students master the Web by presenting a concise introduction to one important Internet topic or technology in each book. The books start from square one and assume no prior experience with the technology being covered. Mastering the Web doesn't come with a wave of a magic wand; but by studying these accessible, highly visual textbooks, readers will be well on their way.

The series is written by instructors who are familiar with the challenges beginners face when learning the material. To this end, the Web Wizard books offer more than a cookbook approach: they emphasize principles and offer clear explanations, giving the reader a strong foundation of knowledge on which to build.

Numerous features highlight important points and aid in learning:

☆ Tips — important points to keep in mind

☆ Shortcuts — timesaving ideas

☆ Warnings — things to watch out for

☆ Flash MX — latest updates to Flash

☆ Review questions and hands-on exercises

☆ Online references — Web sites to visit to obtain more information

Supplementary materials for the books, including updates, additional examples, and source code, are available at `http://www.aw.com/webwizard`. Also available for qualified instructors adopting a book from the series are instructor's manuals, sample tests, and solutions. Please contact your Addison-Wesley sales representative for the instructor resources password.

About This Book

Flash is a popular tool for enriching Web sites. Even though it is a powerful program, it can be fun and easy to learn. From writing tutorials for Webmonkey.com and teaching both professional designers and inexperienced non-designers, I have found that the key to learning how to use Flash is not absorbing every detail of every last feature, but getting down the basics. Many of my students have gone on to be Flash masters in their own right, but I have also learned something important from them—how to teach the basics of Flash successfully. This book will get you creating animations so quickly that you'll be hooked on Flash. From there, you will progress to creating interactivity, adding sound, and building Flash skills advanced enough to let you use it professionally.

At its core, Flash is an animation program. This book provides comprehensive lessons and insights for creating animation, using sound, and publishing Flash movies. However, since the advent of Flash 5, ActionScript has become an essential skill as well. Chapter 7 in this book is unique in providing a solid introduction to ActionScript for newcomers, with a lot less pain than reading through a lengthy reference written just for programmers. After this book, it's up to you continue to practice what you learn, as there is virtually no limit on how far you can go as a Flash Wizard.

> ☆ **FLASH MX**   **This Book Covers Both Flash 5 and Flash MX**
>
> Most of what's changed in Flash MX is the look and feel of the program, not what you create with it. The main text addresses Flash 5, and tip boxes like this one point out the essential changes in Flash MX. Also, some of the figures compare Flash 5 and Flash MX features. If you are using Flash MX, look for these boxes.

Acknowledgments

This book is dedicated to the memory of Ernesto Gerona. I owe thanks to the support and inspiration of more friends, family members, and colleagues than I can mention here. I am particularly grateful to Gary Bernal for his support, astute insight, and for his illustrations which have improved the figures throughout. Jeremy Clark at Macromedia was an essential ally who took time from shepherding the development of Flash MX to answer my endless questions. Deborah Schultz provided invaluable input in my quest to synthesize the vast subject of ActionScript into a single chapter. Evany Thomas and Mike Calore have made my words sing on Webmonkey, the genesis for this book. Marlow Markus, Laura O'Connor, Larry Kay, and Sharan Street have also provided constructive criticism. I owe a lot to members of the Flash community who have been my teachers.

At Addison-Wesley, the editors Susan Hartman Sullivan and Galia Shokry made this all possible and were active partners throughout the entire process. As copyeditor, Kathy Smith ensured this book's readability. The following academic reviewers who have championed the point of view of Flash students were essential in shaping this book:

Craig M. Kapp, The College of New Jersey

Harriet C.W. Thompson, Tulane University College

Vanessa Dennen, San Diego State University

Susan Herrington, Albuquerque TVI

Chris Beaumont, Queens College, Charlotte N.C.

Emily Stern, The College of New Rochelle

Don Anderson, Chadron State College

James Kirk, Western Carolina University

CHAPTER ONE

Getting Started with Flash

Flash is a great way to add rich multimedia content to almost any Web page. With the help of this book, you can begin creating animations in no time, even if you aren't a Web pro or a seasoned animator. You will also be on your way to working with interactivity and sound. This chapter will give you an idea of what Flash does and how it works, and will provide you with an orientation to the program's tools that you will apply in subsequent chapters.

Chapter Objectives

☆ Explain the role of Flash in the Web
☆ Define vector graphics and other characteristics of Flash
☆ Get oriented to the Flash program
☆ Understand how to change the view of the work area and add guides
☆ Set preferences for the Flash program

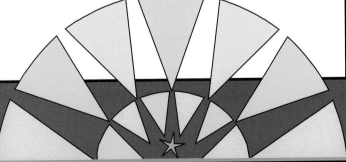

◎◎ What Is Flash?

Flash is a multimedia program that was invented specifically for the Web. Flash began as FutureSplash, which Macromedia acquired in 1997. Flash combines motion, graphics, sound, and interactivity in a format that is efficient on a Web page.

The earliest Web pages were very plain: just text with links on a gray background. That was all that early Web browsers could display (see Figure 1.1). There were no graphics, typefaces, or colors, but this was pretty cool for the time—there had been nothing like that before.

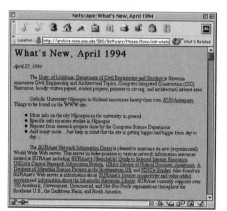

Figure 1.1 Early Web pages were just simple text and links on a gray background (right). Today some sites use Flash to create entertaining graphics and richer experiences (left).

As Web artists saw the potential to do more, from art and entertainment to e-commerce, they clamored for more tools. Static images (those which don't move), colors, and typefaces were added first. Eventually, motion was added in the form of animated GIF images and **Shockwave**. Early Shockwave was revolutionary, but it was rarely used since it required mastering a difficult program (Macromedia Director); in addition, the files were usually too large to be practical on a Web site.

Today, Flash is the most popular program for creating rich Web graphics and multimedia experiences. Flash is relatively easy to use (as you will see), and it tends to create small files which can be viewed by almost any Web browser. Those files are called **Shockwave Flash** or **SWF** (pronounced "swiff") files. As you work through this book, you'll be publishing SWF files and adding them to Web pages.

To display Flash content, a Web user must have installed a special piece of software called a **plug-in** or **player**. The Flash plug-in is free, and 98% of all Web users have some version of it installed. Thus the door is open for nearly everyone to participate in a truly multimedia experience. However, it is not just the popularity of the plug-in that makes Flash a compelling tool.

Vector-Based Graphics

Flash is a **vector-based** graphics program. There are two types of graphic images you can create with a computer: **bitmap** or **vector**. Most Web sites display graphics in one of two bitmap formats, **GIF** or **JPEG**, but the vector format offers a few advantages.

A bitmap graphic (also called **raster** image) is composed of many tiny squares (**pixels**), each a different color, which when viewed together create an illusion that we see as a photograph, logo, or other artwork (see Figure 1.2). You may have noticed pixels if you've ever zoomed in on an image in a graphics program such as Photoshop. Generally, one GIF or JPEG image is made of thousands of pixels.

Behind the scenes, a bitmap image defines the color of each pixel: "Make this pixel this color, that pixel that color, and so on ...." On the other hand, a vector image uses a geometric equation: "Make a circle with this diameter and this color, period." You don't actually need to know geometry since Flash does this for you invisibly, creating smaller files that will load faster in a Web browser.

Another advantage of vector images is their display quality. A vector circle will always look crisp whether it is resized bigger or smaller, even if it's enlarged 100 times (see Figure 1.2). A bitmap circle can be a pretty good circle—but it probably won't look so good if it is enlarged. You could create a giant vector-based map of a large city and allow a viewer to zoom in to see the detail of a single block without losing any clarity.

Figure 1.2 A simulation of the differences between a bitmap circle (left) and a vector circle (right).

Flash emphasizes vector images but also supports bitmap images. Bitmap images are still better at reproducing photographs, while vectors have the edge for rendering type and shapes. In the next chapter, you'll learn how to draw and edit vector artwork and also how to integrate bitmap images.

Flash Files Are Smaller

If you've ever surfed the Web on a slow browser, you probably have noticed how some pages take a lot longer to download (or display) than others. File size is the biggest influence on how fast Web pages display. If you use it well, Flash can create relatively small, easy-to-download files that are rich with animation, sound, and interactivity.

Vector graphics are only one reason why Flash files are small. Throughout this book, you'll learn how to use symbols, streaming, sound compression, and other features to keep those files lean. For the same file size as that picture of your dog, you can create a Flash movie that really moves (see Figure 1.3).

Figure 1.3 Sure, the pup is cute, but you could create sound, motion, and interactivity for the same file size in Flash as Funny Garbage has done with Katbot.com (right).

No More Messy Rollover Script

Simple interactions are a snap. With Flash, you don't need to be a programmer to create animated buttons (called rollovers) or a music player. **ActionScript**, introduced in Chapter Seven, is a relatively accessible programming language just for Flash, and it expands the power of these actions.

Flash Plays Well with Others

You could create everything you need for a project from Flash, but you don't have to. Flash can import sound, image, and movie files. For some specialized tasks such as creating bitmap artwork or sound files, you will need to use other graphics or sound-editing programs and import the work into Flash. Although its built-in tools are quite capable, Flash also works well with other vector-based programs such as Adobe Illustrator and Macromedia Freehand.

Synched Sound Is a Cinch

Flash is the simplest way to add sound to a Web page. You can include a background music track, give a button a "click" sound effect, or add sound to any part of a Flash movie. Flash utilizes MP3 compression, which gives you the best sound quality for the smallest file size. Chapter Five is devoted to using sound in Flash.

◎◎ When (and When Not) to Use Flash

There are various ways to use Flash to enrich a Web site. Its biggest strength is for entertainment. There is no better tool for creating an animated Web cartoon. More advanced users of the program can create compelling games. You can use Flash to create a single illustration or an entire Web site, or buttons to navigate around a site.

Flash is starting to sound so great that you may be tempted to use it everywhere. Well, resist that temptation. Chapter Eight goes into more detail about how to use Flash appropriately, but there is one general rule of thumb you can start with: Think about what you want your Web site to accomplish and ask yourself, "Will Flash make it better or will it just annoy the audience?" Also, resist the temptation to use Flash for everything on a site if it makes more sense to confine its use to a single graphic.

Flash can make a lot of sense for an entertainment or fashion site, but for a mainstream site such as Yahoo.com or CNN.com, it can do more harm than good. Visitors at these sites prefer the more direct experience of a standard HTML Web page.

◎◎ Working with Flash

To use Flash, all you need is a personal computer and a Web browser with the latest version of the Flash plug-in installed. Of course, you'll also need a copy of the Flash program. If you don't have a copy of Flash and aren't sure about buying it yet, Macromedia, the maker of Flash, provides a free 30-day trial from its Web site. Once you've installed Flash, you should have everything you need.

If you are familiar with another graphics program such as Adobe Illustrator, Adobe Photoshop, Macromedia Fireworks, or Macromedia Freehand, that's great. And if you know how to use a sound-editing program such as SoundForge, you're way ahead of most of us.

While using Flash, you'll be creating two kinds of files. Each can be identified by a 3-letter suffix, called an **extension**. The work document or file (named like this: "filename.*fla*") is where you do your work. These files can be opened only with the Flash program. From there you create, or publish, a second kind of file, the SWF file (named like this: "filename.*swf*"). The SWF files play in the Web browser. (Chapter Six covers publishing SWF files.) In each case, you should append the corresponding .*fla* or .*swf* to the filename.

☆ **WARNING** File Formats and Their Extensions

The Web uses what are called **file extensions** to identify different types of files. A file extension is a period or dot followed by a standard three-to-four-character abbreviation. It's appended to the end of a filename (e.g., *index.html*, *picture.gif*, *movie.swf*). A standard Web page is an HTML file with the extension .*html* or .*htm*; a GIF image uses .*gif*; and a Shockwave Flash file ends with .*swf*. These extensions are required for files to work properly on a Web site.

Windows (and Macintosh OS X) may hide these extensions from you, but they are still there. When developing content for the Web, it's best to reveal these extensions. These settings are outside of the Flash program in the computer's operating system. In Windows, open the Folder Options control panel and uncheck *Hide file extensions for known file types*. In Macintosh OS X, choose Finder→Preferences and check *Always show file extensions* (see Figure 1.4).

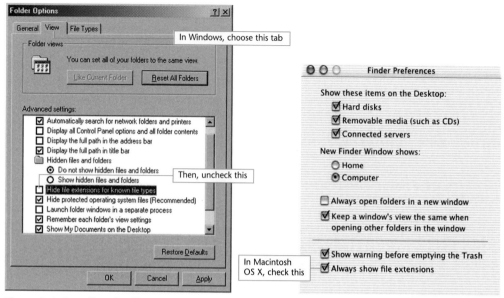

Figure 1.4 Revealing the file name extensions in Windows (left) and Macintosh OS X (right).

◎◎ A Tour of the Flash Program

There are four main parts to the Flash program. First, there's the **Stage** where you assemble what's seen in the Flash movie. Accompanying the Stage is the **Timeline**, where you determine what happens and when. Most of the controls for changing what happens on the Stage and Timeline are in the **Panels**. You may be familiar with the **Menu Bar** in other programs. In Flash, the Menu Bar appears at the top of the window and displays categories of commands such as "File→New" or "Edit→Preferences."

The Stage

The Stage is your workspace. Draw, select, and position artwork here. The Stage represents what will be visible in the final Flash movie that you will export (the SWF file). Although it's not a perfect preview of your work, it displays placed elements and how they change according to the Timeline.

At the top of the Stage is the name of the file you're currently working on. At the top left is the name of the current scene or symbol that appears on the Stage. At the top right are shortcuts for accessing other symbols and scenes. (See Figure 1.5.)

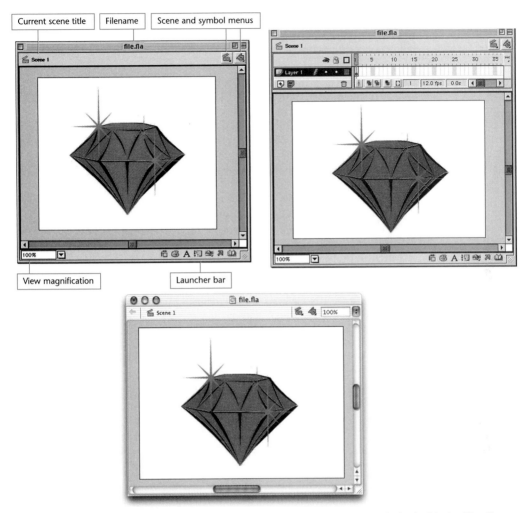

Figure 1.5 The Stage alone is at the top left. At the top right is the Stage docked with the Timeline. Below is the Flash MX Stage in Macintosh OS X.

The Timeline

As the name implies, the Timeline represents what is happening to your movie over time. Here you'll apply animation, interactivity, and sounds.

Each frame, indicated by hash marks from left to right, represents an increment of time. The moveable red frame indicator (also called the **playhead**) determines which frame is active on the Stage. Special frames called **keyframes** (introduced in Chapter Three) mark changed views on the Stage. Various dots, arrows, comments, and other markings indicate what is happening from frame to frame.

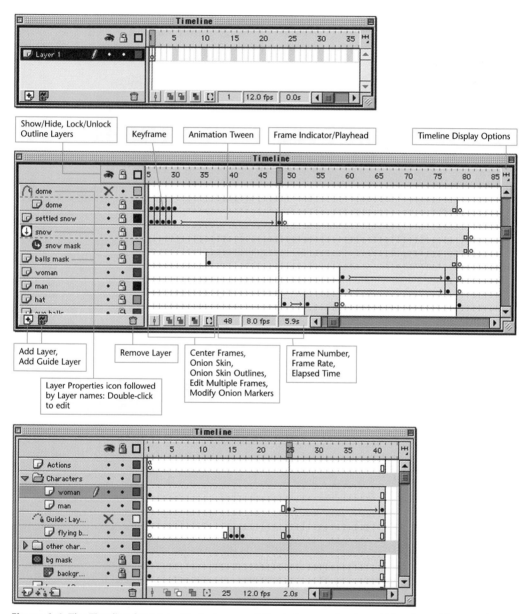

Figure 1.6 The Timeline for a new Flash document (top). A more developed Timeline with many layers and frames (center). The Flash MX Timeline (bottom).

Layers are an organizational device. Use them to separate graphics, animation, sound, and actions on the Stage and Timeline. Objects placed in one layer will appear in front of objects placed in other layers. Chapter Two covers layers in more detail.

At the bottom of the Timeline are a few buttons. The first will center the current frame in the Timeline. The others are for the **onion skin** feature (covered in Chapter Three), which allows you to view or edit multiple frames at once. In Figure 1.6, the numbers to the right of these buttons indicate the current frame (48), the frame rate (8.0 frames per second), and how much time has elapsed up to the current frame (5.9 seconds).

☆ **TIP**   **The Stage and the Timeline: Together or á la Carte?**

The Timeline and Stage are interrelated, so it is best to use them as one unit (see Figure 1.5). If you want them apart, click and drag the Timeline away from the Stage. To dock (join) them, drag and release the Timeline over an edge of the Stage.

Panels

The panels are small windows that float in the Flash workspace. Each panel has controls dedicated to specific tasks such as selecting tools, changing colors, or composing actions. Open panels from the Window menu.

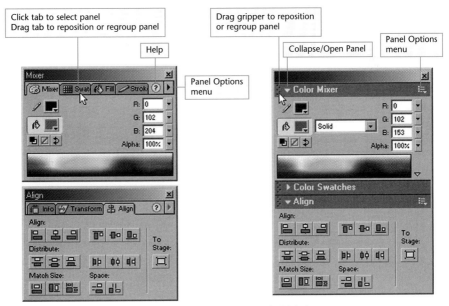

Figure 1.7 A few Flash 5 panels (left). Flash MX panels (right).

☆ FLASH MX   A New Look for Panels

One of the most obvious changes in Flash MX is the look of the panels. (See Figure 1.7.) The tabs are eliminated in favor of gripper handles and collapsing controls. You can move each panel and dock it by its gripper. Collapse or expand a panel by clicking on the triangle on the left. In Windows, you can drag panels to the left or right edge of the Flash work area to anchor them there.

The upper right corner of most panels has a triangle and a ? symbol. Click on the triangle to reveal more options for that panel. If you want to learn more about a particular panel or tool, click on the ? symbol to get specific help. Several of the panels have white boxes for text input where you designate properties such as line thickness or typeface. These input boxes usually are accompanied by sliders and menus, so you don't have to remember exactly what to type.

You can group the panels in Flash to suit the way you work. You can sort all of the color panels as one group and the text panels as another. To do this, just drag one panel's tab and release it on top of another panel's tab. To separate them, drag one panel's tab away from those of the other panels.

Once you have opened several panels the way you prefer them, you can save that arrangement. Choose Save Panel Layout from the Window menu and name it something like *my set*. Anytime after that, you can select *my set* from the Window→Panel Sets submenu to instantly rearrange the panels to the saved arrangement.

☆ SHORTCUT   Hiding Panels with the ⌞Tab⌟ Key

Sometimes you will find yourself focusing on the Stage and you will need as much space as possible. With all of these panels, your desktop can get pretty cluttered. Press the ⌞Tab⌟ key on your keyboard to hide all of the panels at once. Press the ⌞Tab⌟ key again to reveal them just as they were. This is quicker than closing panels one by one, and you won't have to remember which panels were previously opened. ⌞Ctrl⌟-⌞Alt⌟-⌞T⌟ (⌞⌘⌟-⌞Option⌟-⌞T⌟ for Macintosh) will hide or reveal the Timeline.

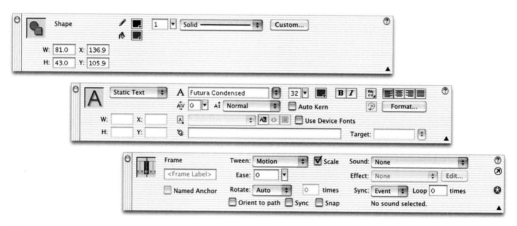

Figure 1.8   The Properties Inspector in Flash MX changes according to what you have selected.

☆ **FLASH MX**   **Properties Inspector**

Flash MX changes the way you access attributes of frames and placed objects. Several of the panels from version 5 have been removed and replaced by the **Properties Inspector** (see Figure 1.8). This is a big improvement. Rather than shuffling through several panels to change an attribute, select an object and go to the Properties Inspector.

The Properties Inspector changes according to whatever object you have selected. If you select a drawn shape, attributes such as color and size will be available. If you select text, it will allow you to choose a typeface. A selected frame will also access animation settings.

Menu Bar

Like any other program, Flash's menu bar at the top of the screen gives you access to many of its features (see Figure 1.9). Some of the menu items are redundant to controls on other panels, but some are only available here. Click on a top category and pull down a menu to select from a list of commands.

Many of these menu items, or commands, are referred to throughout this book in this format: File→Open. The command starts with the main menu's name (e.g., Modify), and may be followed by a submenu (e.g., Modify→Transform), and ends with the command to be selected (e.g., Modify→Transform→Scale and Rotate).

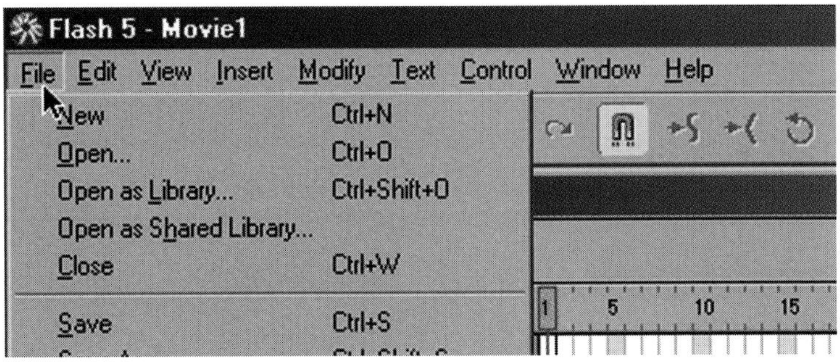

Figure 1.9 The Flash 5 menu bar with the File menus revealed (Windows version).

☆ **TIP**   **Keyboard Shortcuts**

Most menu items have keyboard shortcuts. These shortcuts can save you time for commands that you use frequently. They are displayed alongside the menu items so that you can easily remember just the ones you want (e.g., Ctrl-O [Windows] or ⌘-O [Macintosh] next to the File→Open command).

Not every command has a shortcut. If you want to assign a shortcut for something such as Insert→Layer, you can add it from Edit→Keyboard Shortcuts.

Pop-up Commands and Tooltips

Right-click ([Ctrl]-click for Macintosh) on a frame in the Timeline, on an object on the Stage, or on almost anything and a **contextual menu** will pop up. This pop-up menu offers several items specific to what you are clicking on. Choose any option from that menu.

Let the mouse hover over an icon in the Flash program and a **tooltip** will pop up to identify it. (See Figure 1.10.) If the tooltips annoy you, disable them by unchecking *Show Tooltips* in the preferences (Edit→Preferences).

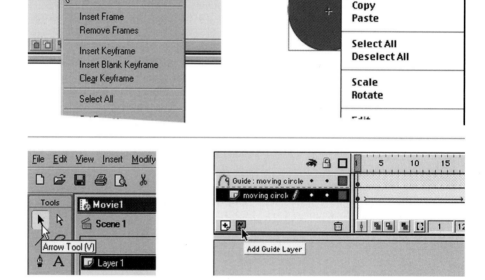

Figure 1.10 Pop-up contextual menus (top) and tooltips (bottom).

◎◎ Changing the View

While you are working, you may need to zoom in to see some detail or to overlay a grid to align multiple objects. Various tools and menu commands allow you to alter the view of the Stage.

☆ **WARNING** The View Does Not Affect Exported SWF Files

All of these tools and techniques help you while you work in the Flash program. They have no effect on the final Flash movie (SWF file) that you publish.

Changing the View

View Tools

While working in Flash, you probably won't be content to always view the entire Stage at the widest view. You may need to zoom in to work on a detail, and then you may need to move to another area of the Stage. There are two tools for this under the View section of the Tools panel.

The **Zoom Tool** allows you to enlarge the view of the Stage area. From the Tools panel, select the Zoom tool (see Figure 1.11). Just click it on the Stage to zoom in (or enlarge) where you click. Click multiple times to enlarge the view even more. Click-drag to define a rectangular marquee and release, and the view will zoom to the area you selected. To zoom out (or reduce the view), hold down the [Option] key on your keyboard before you click with the Zoom tool.

To move around the Stage, you can click on the standard scroll bars and sliders on the edge of the window, or use the **Hand** tool. Choose the Hand tool and the cursor becomes a hand. Just like you would with artwork on your desk, click-down and drag the hand in the Stage area to reposition the view of the work area.

☆ SHORTCUT **Toggling to the Zoom or Hand Tool**

From almost any other tool, you can toggle to the Hand tool with the [Spacebar] on your keyboard. Hold down the [Spacebar] and [Ctrl] keys ([Spacebar] and [⌘] keys for Macintosh) to toggle to the Zoom tool. When you release the keys, the previously selected tool will still be selected. These shortcuts won't work with the Text tool.

What's the Magnification?

The current magnification is displayed at the bottom-left corner of the Stage (see Figure 1.11). In Flash MX, it's in the upper-right corner. 100% is the size that the published movie would normally be displayed in a Web browser window. Anything less than 100% gives you a wider (or smaller) view with less detail. A value greater than 100% gives a larger, close-up view. To zoom to an exact percentage, type a number right there and then hit the [Enter] key on your keyboard. Pull down the menu right next to the percentage box for preset values.

The View Menu

You can change the magnification of the Stage from the View menu as well. **Zoom In** and **Zoom Out** work just like the Zoom tool. The **Magnification** submenu allows you to zoom to selected views.

There are four View modes that affect the quality and speed of the display in Flash.

☆ **Outlines** give the fastest performance but the crudest preview. This mode will display only the outline of all objects, but no fill color. It also is a convenient way to display the boundaries of each object when you have trouble distinguishing them.

Changing the View

☆ **Fast** gives you a better preview of the Stage, but the objects will appear jagged.

☆ **Antialias** gives all drawn objects smoother edges, but text will still appear jagged.

☆ **Antialias Text** gives the best appearance. The edges of all objects and text will appear smooth. This mode may cause objects to display more slowly.

There's a trade-off: The smoother the view, the slower the performance. If possible, use the Antialias Text setting. If you have to wait too long for the image to redraw each time you scroll, try the Antialias or Fast setting.

When the **Work Area** option is checked under the View menu, the gray work area surrounding the Stage area is visible. Any objects placed off stage will be visible too. If this option is disabled (unchecked in the menu), only what is in the Stage area is visible. This is how the Stage will be framed when published. Since both modes are useful at times, you'll probably use this feature often. Enabling this option makes it easier to move objects around, but disabling it gives a better preview of your work.

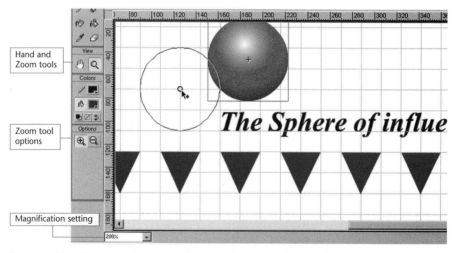

Figure 1.11 Aligning objects with the Ruler, Guides, and Grids. The Zoom and Hand tools are outlined in red.

Rulers, Guides, and Grids

In many cases, you may feel comfortable aligning objects by eye, but other times, you may want to be more exact than that. Select the View→Rulers option and two rulers will appear at the top and left side of the Stage (see Figure 1.11). These rulers are a reference for positioning and aligning objects. Click on either ruler and drag a **guide** onto the Stage. Drag an existing guide to reposition it; or drag it into a ruler to remove it.

Once you have placed any guides, you can hide or lock them under the View→Guides submenu.

☆ Uncheck View→Guides→Show Guides to clean up your work area.

☆ Select View→Guides→Lock Guides to be sure that you don't move any guides unintentionally.

☆ If View→Guides→Snap to Guides is checked, it will help you to magnetically align objects to the guides, even if the guides are hidden.

The **grid** works a lot like guides, except that it covers the entire Stage, like graph paper. You can show or hide the grid, and turn its Snap to feature on or off.

☆ You cannot move the grid, but from View→Grid→Edit Grid, you can change its spacing.

☆ Check View→Grid→Snap to Grid and uncheck *Show Grid*; and the grid will invisibly help you align everything in the Flash movie.

☆ **FLASH MX   Snap to Pixels**

If you are using Flash MX, choose the View→Snap to Pixels option. Computer displays do not tend to display objects as well if they are placed between pixels. The effect of this option may seem subtle, but it ensures that your artwork is aligned at exact pixels and will improve its appearance.

◎◉ Setting Preferences

The preferences allow you to adapt the Flash program to the way you like to work (see Figure 1.12). Once you are more comfortable with Flash, you can try altering some of the settings and see what works for you. Several preference options are discussed below.

General

☆ **Undo levels**: Controls how far you can go back to undo your work. Press Ctrl-Z (⌘-Z on a Macintosh) repeatedly to undo your work one action at a time. A larger number will allow more undos, but will use more memory.

☆ **Shift Select**: Mimics the bad interface of Flash 3 and before. Leave this checked.

☆ **Timeline Options**: Make keyframes in the Timeline easier to identify and manipulate. Check *Flash 4 Frame Drawing* and *Flash 4 Selection Style*. In Flash MX, leave the Timeline options *unchecked*.

☆ **Highlight Color**: Colors active selections. Each object can be highlighted according to its layer's assigned color or all objects are highlighted with the same color.

☆ **Actions Panel Mode**: Affects format of Actions panel. You can change this to Expert Mode when you get to Chapter Seven.

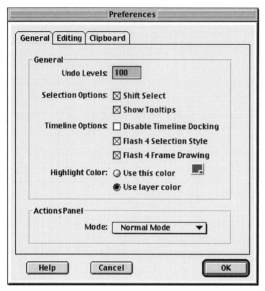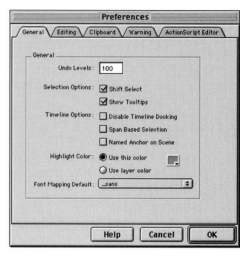

Figure 1.12 Preferences windows for Flash 5 and Flash MX.

Editing

Pen Tool

These options affect the display of object paths while using the Pen tool.

☆ **Show Pen Preview**: Shows how a line will look before you click with the Pen tool.

☆ **Show Solid Points**: If checked, unselected points will appear solid, and selected ones hollow. If unchecked, the opposite will be true.

☆ **Show Precise Cursors**: Changes pen cursor from pen to crosshairs.

Drawing Settings

The Pencil tool uses automatic features to help you draw straight lines and smooth curves. These settings allow you to adjust those automatic features.

Clipboard Settings

Bitmaps and Gradients (PICT Settings for Macintosh)

You can copy artwork between Flash and other programs. These settings affect how bitmap images translate between Flash and the other programs.

Freehand Text

Keep *Maintain Text as Blocks* checked. Otherwise imported blocks of text will be broken into separate lines.

☆ **FLASH MX**   **New Preference Settings**

Two new tabs have been added to the Preference options in Flash MX. The ActionScript Editor settings affect the appearance of scripts in the Actions panel. The Warnings settings help you prevent mistakes. Leave these settings alone until you are more comfortable with using Flash. For a detailed description of all the settings, consult the Flash MX Help.

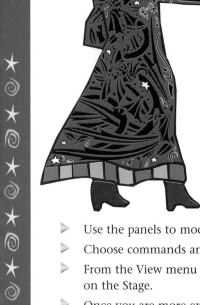

☆ Summary

▷ Macromedia Flash is a great way to enrich Web pages with motion, sound, and interactivity.

▷ Vector graphics generally create smaller files and look sharp at any size.

▷ Use Flash appropriately. Some sites can use Flash everywhere, while others should use it infrequently or not at all.

▷ The Stage is the work area.

▷ The Timeline influences what happens in the Flash movie over time.

▷ Use the panels to modify settings or select tools.

▷ Choose commands and settings from the menu bar.

▷ From the View menu you can change magnification or add guides to help align objects on the Stage.

▷ Once you are more experienced with Flash, you can change the Preferences to suit the way you work.

☆ Online References

Download the Latest Flash Plug-in
`http://www.macromedia.com/shockwave/download/index.cgi?P1_Prod_Version=ShockwaveFlash`

Flash 30-day Free Trial Download
`http://www.macromedia.com/software/flash/trial`

Macromedia Help Site
`http://www.macromedia.com/support/flash`

Flashkit Resource Site
`http://www.flashkit.com`

FlashLite Resource Site
`http://www.flashlite.net`

We're Here Flash Forums
`http://www.were-here.com`

Flasher List: Join and learn from your peers
`http://www.chinwag.com/flasher`

Webmonkey Flash 5 Tutorial
http://www.webmonkey.com/multimedia/shockwave_flash/
tutorials/tutorial8.html

Bitmap versus Vector Graphics
http://users.belgacom.net/prepresspanic/image/
bitmapvector.htm

Flash Plug-in Statistics
http://www.macromedia.com/software/flash/survey

☆ Review Questions

1. Explain the difference between a bitmap image and a vector image. Which one does Flash emphasize?

2. List two reasons why Flash is popular.

3. Which Flash file format do you use to do your work? Which one do you use to publish in a Web page? Give an example of a filename for each format.

4. What is a filename extension? Why is it important?

5. Where in Flash do you draw and position artwork?

6. Where in Flash do you add frames (and time) to a movie?

7. What do you use to separate elements and place one object in front of another?

8. If you don't remember it, where can you find the keyboard shortcut for the *Insert Keyframe* command?

9. From which menu do you open the panels? Under which menu is the *Flip Horizontal* command?

10. List two features that help you align objects. Describe how they work.

☆ Hands-On Exercises

1. Launch the Flash program and use the command File→New to start a new work document. Be intuitive with the program. Without worrying about what you are doing, experiment with the tools and panels to see what happens.

2. Go to http://www.animationexpress.com and http://www.macromedia.com/software/flash/special/inspiration/. Look at different examples that were created in Flash. Pick two that you like. Explain what you like about them.

3. Go the the Flash area of the Web Wizard Web site (http://www.aw.com/webwizard). Download the link *Chapter 1 Exercises*. Open the file called *tryout.fla* and look at the Timeline and Stage. Move the frame indicator back and forth to see how the frames change. Hide different layers to see what that does.

4. Close all of the panels on the right side of the Stage. Open the following panels: Swatches, Mixer, Info, Align, Transform. Group these panels and arrange them the way you like in your workspace. Use Window→Save Panel Layout to save this arrangement. Choose Window→Panel Sets→Default Layout and see what happens to the panels. Next, choose the panel layout that you saved from the same menu.

5. Open the same file you downloaded for Exercise 3. From the View menu, change the display to Antialias, Fast, Outlines, and back to Antialias Text. Observe how each setting affects the display of the Stage. Reveal the rulers, guides, and grids. Use the Zoom tool to magnify the view and then zoom back out.

CHAPTER TWO

CREATING GRAPHICS

Flash has several robust drawing features. You can create most graphics without ever leaving the program, even with type. And if you prefer the features of another graphics program, Flash supports that too. To really understand these tools, you'll have to try them out yourself. Experiment and you'll discover there's usually more than one way to do the same thing.

Chapter Objectives

- ☆ Set up and save a work document
- ☆ Become familiar with the drawing tools
- ☆ Select and manipulate artwork
- ☆ Manage the color of objects
- ☆ Use layers effectively
- ☆ Import images from other sources
- ☆ Create and modify text

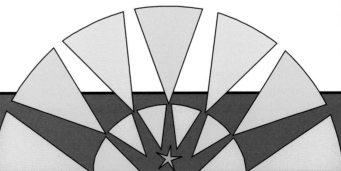

◉◉ Creating New Files and Saving Your Work

You create and save Flash documents much like documents in other computer programs. Whenever you need to start from scratch, choose the New option from the File menu. Choose File→Open to work with an existing Flash file. And always, always use the File→Save option.

While you are working, save as often as possible, ideally every few minutes. Use the shortcut Ctrl-S (⌘-S for Macintosh). This will protect your work from a computer crash or other unexpected event. As insurance, once a day, copy your files to a backup disk. Your computer could be completely dead tomorrow, but your work would not be lost.

Use the File→Save As command to save a new version of your Flash file. Rename the new file and it will leave the last saved file untouched while creating multiple versions of your work. You can name the files sequentially to help keep track of which version is the latest (e.g., file1.fla, file2.fla, file3.fla). From a newer version, you can experiment to your heart's delight, and if you don't like what happens, you can always start over with an older version.

☆ FLASH MX   Save As Flash 5

If you're lucky enough to be using Flash MX, you can still share your working Flash document with others who are using Flash 5. From the File→Save As window, choose *Flash 5 Document* as the Format. This will save your work in a format that can be opened by Flash 5. Under Edit→Preferences be sure that *Warn on Save for Macromedia Flash 5 compatibility* is checked in the Warnings view. This will alert you if you've used a Flash MX-only feature.

☆ TIP   When Flash Cannot Open the File

At times you'll come across a Flash file that just won't open, and you know it should. This occurs frequently with the Macintosh version of Flash when you download a file from the Web or receive it from someone who uses the Windows version of Flash.

There's a simple way to work around this. From the File→Open window there is a file browser and a menu of file types. If you can't see the file that you want to open there, change the file type to *All Files* (not *All Formats*). This allows you to select any file on your computer. Find the Flash file this way and it should open. This also will work when you import bitmap images or sound files.

◉◉ Setting Movie Properties

Movie Properties settings apply to the entire Flash movie. When creating a Flash file, choose Modify→Movie. Here, you can specify the following:

☆ **Frame Rate**: Designate frames per second (fps), how many frames will play over one second of time.

☆ **Dimensions**: Specify the width and height of the Stage.

☆ **Background Color**: Click here to pick a color that will show behind all objects on the Stage.

☆ **Ruler Units**: Choose how you measure objects in Flash. *Pixels* are the preferred choice for Web projects.

At any time, you can come back to these settings to change them. However, you should think carefully about the frame rate and dimensions at the start of your project. Since they affect the timing and composition of the movie respectively, changing either one drastically later on may require you to reposition many frames and objects.

The ideal frame rate is a subject of debate. The higher the frame rate, the more frames are needed for each second of playing time. There are several other factors to consider:

☆ A higher frame rate allows for smoother animation.

☆ A lower frame rate tends to create a smaller file size because there are fewer frames.

☆ Some frame rates perform more consistently on different computers. 20 fps does not display 20 frames in a second for everyone, but 31 fps comes close.

☆ Other frame rates work better with heavy-duty ActionScripts.

Some say 12 fps is the best overall setting, others say 24 fps, and still others prefer 31 fps. Somewhere from 8 to 32 fps will generally work best. The right answer is what works best when you test your work. (We will discuss this in Chapter Six.)

☆ **FLASH MX**   **Document Properties**

In Flash MX, the Movie Properties settings are identical, but they are renamed *Document Properties*. The command is Modify→Document. Also, when nothing is selected on the Stage or Timeline, you can access these same settings via the Properties Inspector.

◎◎ Overview of the Tools Panel

The Tools panel (see Figure 2.1) is essential for drawing and manipulating objects in Flash. It normally appears at the left side of your Flash window, but you can drag it anywhere you like. If you don't see the Tools panel, you can reveal it (or hide it) from Window→Tools.

This panel is organized into four labeled sections. The **Tools** section is used for drawing and selecting. **View** is used to change the magnification or position of the Stage work area. Use **Colors** to specify colors. At the bottom of the panel, the **Options** vary depending on which tool you have chosen. The options for some tools are described in this chapter.

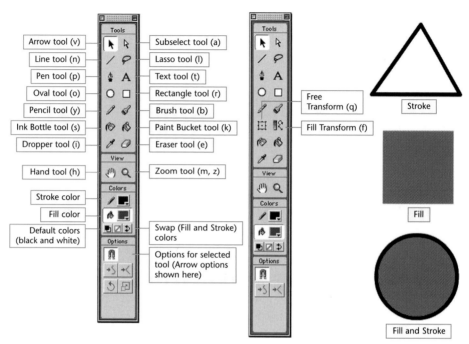

Figure 2.1 The Tools panels for Flash 5 (left) and Flash MX (center). Any object you draw with these tools has a stroke, a fill, or both (right).

◎◎ Drawing in Flash

Drawing in Flash is fairly straightforward. For basic drawing, use the **Pencil**, **Brush**, or **Pen** tool. Choose one of them and start clicking and dragging around in the Stage. That's essentially all you need to do to draw in Flash.

Every shape in Flash can have a **fill** or **stroke**, or both (see Figure 2.1). The fill is the solid area inside a shape. The stroke outlines a shape. The Brush tool creates fill shapes, and the Pencil tool creates strokes. The Pen tool can create shapes with both a stroke and a fill.

☆ **SHORTCUT   The Undo Command**

Never be afraid of making a mistake in Flash. Anything you draw, erase, delete, or change in any way can be undone with a simple keystroke. Choose the Edit→Undo command (Ctrl-Z for Windows or ⌘-Z for Macintosh) and the last brush stroke you painted, the last object you moved, or anything else you did in Flash will be undone as if it never happened. You can repeat this command to undo more than one successive modification.

The Pencil Tool

Use the Pencil tool to draw straight and curved lines. Click and move the mouse in any direction on the Stage; it doesn't have to be straight unless you want it that way.

Can you draw a perfect circle or a straight line? If not, the Pencil tool can help. Under the **Options** section of the Tools panel, you can set the Pencil to one of three modes (see Figure 2.2).

☆ *Straighten* helps you draw straight lines and geometric shapes, even circles. Hold down the (Shift) key on your keyboard to draw perfectly horizontal or vertical lines.

☆ The *Smooth* mode keeps your lines curved.

☆ *Ink* applies almost no modification to your lines. If you stagger, the line will stagger with you.

You don't have to draw an entire line in one motion. You can extend a line with the Pencil tool. Starting from one end of an existing line segment, draw where you want to extend it.

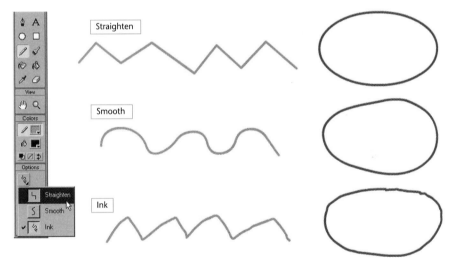

Figure 2.2 Using the Straighten, Smooth, and Ink modes for the Pencil tool.

The Brush Tool

The Pencil tool creates a line with a consistent thickness, a stroke. Use the Brush tool to create a solid shape, a fill. Just click down the mouse and draw in the Stage. As you paint with the Brush tool, all touching or overlapping shapes of the same color will merge into a single shape (see Figure 2.11).

The Brush tool has several options:

★ The Brush Mode affects how the brush mingles with existing shapes. For example, *Paint Behind* will prevent your brush stroke from covering up any other colors. You'll love *Paint Inside* if you had trouble coloring in the lines when you were a kid. It will confine your drawing to the inside or outside of an existing stroke.

★ *Brush Size* and *Brush Shape* are self-explanatory. Choose an option from each of these menus to change the size or shape of the brush.

★ *Lock Fill* is used for painting with a gradient or bitmap image. Covered later in this chapter, a gradient fill uses a range of color shades and Lock Fill will keep those shades in a single position.

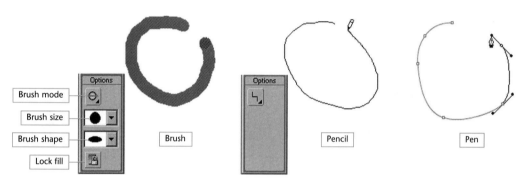

Figure 2.3 Drawing with the Brush, Pencil, and Pen tools.

The Pen Tool

If you are familiar with a vector-based program such as Adobe Illustrator or Macromedia Freehand, you may recognize the Pen tool. Sometimes it's called the **bezier** tool, which is the name of the paths it creates with points and handles. Use this tool to draw lines and shapes by clicking and dragging from point to point.

If you're satisfied with the Pencil and Brush tools, you don't have to use the Pen tool. But if you draw a lot, it may be worth the practice to learn how to use it. Resources for learning how to use this tool are listed in the Online References section of this chapter.

★**TIP**   **Switching Between Tools**

Flash is a unique vector-drawing program that offers more than one tool for creating vector art. Just forget which shapes you created with what tool—it won't make a difference. The Pen tool creates the same objects that you draw with the Pencil or Brush tools. You can switch between the more intuitive Brush tool and the more precise Pen tool to create a single shape or object.

Adding a Fill or Stroke

You can add, remove, or edit the stroke or fill of any existing shape. With the **Ink Bottle** tool, click on any fill shape to add a stroke to it. Click on an existing stroke to change it. The **Paint Bucket** tool can add a fill shape inside a stroke. To remove a fill or stroke, select it and hit the ⌐Del⌐ key on your keyboard.

The Paint Bucket tool only works with a *closed* stroke. A closed stroke defines a specific shape and has no beginning or end point. A stroke in the shape of the letter C is open and cannot be filled by this tool. A circle-shaped stroke has no beginning or end point, completely surrounding an area inside it. This can be filled by the Paint Bucket.

Try using the Pencil tool to draw one closed shape and another that isn't. Click inside each shape with the Paint Bucket tool to see the difference. If there's a small break (gap) in the shape, change the *Gap Size* option to force the Paint Bucket to ignore it.

Figure 2.4 Filling shapes with the Paint Bucket tool.

In Figure 2.4, the green circle stroke is easily filled by the Paint Bucket tool. The spiral in the middle is an open shape with very large gaps—not a closed shape—so it cannot be filled by the Paint Bucket. The flower shape has smaller gaps that can be ignored depending on the Gap Size option.

Other Drawing Tools

The **Oval** and **Rectangle** tools are fairly straightforward. Click and drag them on the Stage to create a circular or rectangular shape. These tools create shapes with both a fill *and* a stroke. Hold down the ⌐Shift⌐ key on your keyboard to constrain the shapes to either a circle or a square.

Use the **Line Tool** to draw straight line segments. Click down where you want the line to start and drag to where you want it to end. Let go and you have a straight line. If you want a perfectly vertical or horizontal line, hold down the Shift button on your keyboard while using this tool.

The **Eraser Tool** is the opposite of the Brush tool. It removes (erases) anything you drag it over, both fills and strokes. From this tool's options, the *Eraser Mode* can limit it to erasing just fills or strokes. The *Eraser Shape* option offers different sizes and shapes for the Eraser. Double-click on the Eraser tool to clear everything on the Stage.

◎◎ Selecting and Editing Artwork

The first chapter emphasized the advantages of vector graphics in conserving file size. They also are easier to edit. What you draw in Flash, various strokes and fills are referred to as **objects**. Any contiguous shape or collection of shapes, is an object that you can edit.

Each Flash object is defined by its **attributes**. Size, position, color, and shape are some attributes. Click on a vector object and then move it, copy it, or resize it. It's usually a simple technique. And since you are only changing a single attribute at a time, you can easily change that attribute back later on.

By contrast, to change a color in most bitmap programs, you may have to completely redraw an area of the image. To change a color just a little bit, the color of every last pixel is changed. It's nearly impossible to revert your changes later on.

In Flash you never need to fuss too much about creating the perfect shape on first try. You can edit an existing object at any time. From small tweaks to radical changes, there are tools and panels for modifying any object.

Using the Selection Tools

To alter an object in Flash, you need to let the program know what you want to modify by selecting it. Selecting an object makes it active and allows you to move or transform it in a number of ways. (This is true in any graphics program; just the tools might be different.) After selecting an object or part of an object, you can apply effects or colors to it, move or reshape it, copy or delete it.

Arrow Tool

The most essential tool, the **Arrow** tool, is active by default whenever you launch Flash. It's used for selecting, reshaping, moving, and deleting objects. Select an object on the Stage with the Arrow tool before applying any effect to it.

To use the Arrow tool, you don't necessarily need to choose it from the Tools panel. From most other tools, hold down the ⎈Ctrl key (⌘ key for Macintosh) to temporarily toggle to the Arrow tool. After you release the key, the previously active tool will be yours again.

To select with the Arrow tool:

☆ Click on a single object to select it (see Figure 2.5, A).

☆ Click down and drag diagonally to define a rectangle **marquee** that selects an area (see Figure 2.5, B).

☆ Hold down the Shift key on your keyboard and click on multiple objects to select them all at once.

☆ Double-click on a stroke to select the entire stroke.

☆ Double-click on the fill of an object to also select its stroke (if it has one).

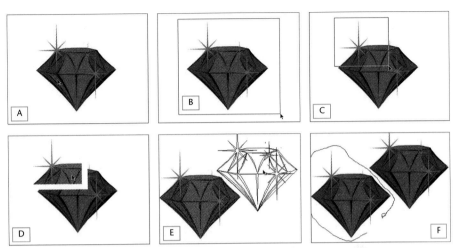

Figure 2.5 Different ways to make a selection.

☆**WARNING Be Sure of What You Have Selected**

When you click and drag diagonally to select an area, Flash will select only what is completely inside the selection area (see Figure 2.5, C). If you don't select enough, you may inadvertently move or transform only part of an object (see Figure 2.5, D). This may be different from what you are used to in other programs. In Flash, it's safest to select objects by clicking and Shift-clicking on objects when it is practical.

Once an object is selected, you can do the following and more:

☆ Drag and move the selection.

☆ Press the Del key on your keyboard to remove the selection.

☆ Copy the selection to the clipboard (Edit→Copy), and paste it somewhere (Edit→Paste).

☆ Duplicate the selection by holding down the Alt key (Option key for Macintosh) while you drag the selection (see Figure 2.5, E).

☆ Apply settings or commands from a panel or menu item.

☆ Use the Arrow tool modifiers (see the next section).

There are a few options for the Arrow tool that change how it behaves. These are available at the bottom of the Tools panel when the Arrow tool is active:

☆ The *Snap to Objects* feature helps to magnetically align one object to another. When you drag or reshape an object from certain points, a small ring will appear. With this option on, the ring will get larger and bolder when it can snap to (align with) another object.

☆ The *Smooth* button smooths the edges of selected objects and rounds them off. You can click more than once to increase the effect.

☆ The *Straighten* button straightens the edges of all the objects in the selection. You can also click this button more than once to increase the effect.

☆ While an object is selected, use the *Rotate* option and the selection will sprout small circular handles. Click and drag on these handles to rotate or skew the selected object.

☆ When you choose the *Scale* option, the selection will sprout small square handles. Move these handles to resize the object.

Without selecting it, you can reshape an object with the Arrow tool. Click and drag an edge or corner to reshape it. Be sure the object isn't selected first, or this won't work (see Figure 2.6).

☆ **FLASH MX   Free Transform Tool**

Flash MX introduces the **Free Transform** tool. This replaces the Scale and Rotate modifiers from the Flash 5 Arrow tool and adds more control for distorting ungrouped objects. Click this tool on an object and it will sprout a frame with handles. You can resize, rotate, and distort an object by moving the various handles and sides of the frame.

You can modify the behavior of this tool for each selection. Drag the center point (the hollow circle in the center) of the object to change the axis of the transformations. The options for this tool (at the bottom of the Tools panel) allow you to distort a selected object in a few different ways. The Envelope option is a more free form distortion. Go ahead; try it out.

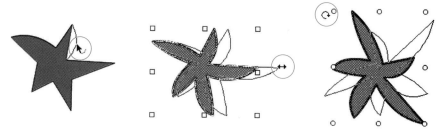

Figure 2.6 Reshaping (left), scaling (center), and rotating (right) an object.

Lasso Tool

Not everything you want to select fits in a rectangle. The **Lasso** tool allows you to make an irregular selection (see Figure 2.5, F). Just click and drag in any path and it will select the area you describe. You can move or delete what you select or modify it with another tool.

Subselect Tool

Flash lets you manipulate lines and shapes in two different ways. Remember the Pen tool? It's different from the other drawing tools in that it uses points and handles. The **Subselect** tool allows you to reshape any object, but with the points and handles of the Pen tool.

☆**TIP**   **Adding to and Subtracting from Selections**

After you make a selection in Flash, you can add to the selection by depressing the ⬚Shift key on the keyboard. Even if you started with the Arrow tool and switched to the Lasso tool, you can combine those selections. ⬚Shift-click on an unselected object to add it to the selection. ⬚Shift-click again on a selected object to drop it from the selection.

Object Panels

Flash has three panels that can modify or transform selected objects on the Stage. A lot of what they do is the same as what you can do with the Arrow tool options, but with more accuracy. Once you have selected a single object or multiple objects, you can modify them from these panels (see Figure 2.7).

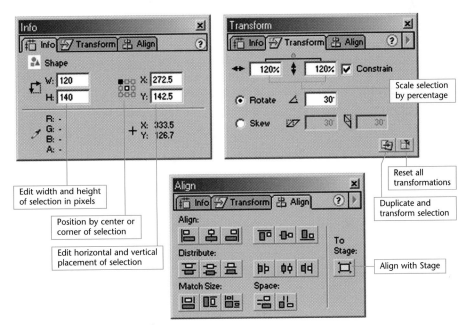

Figure 2.7 The object panels.

Info

Change the position or size of an object by typing in different values in pixels. The bottom half of the window gives you feedback on where the cursor is and what color is under it.

Transform

Resize the selection by percentage. Rotate it or skew it by degree angles. Enter numerical values in the white input fields. In the bottom right corner is a button that will undo all of the transformations.

Align

Use this panel to precisely align or space out multiple objects. Select more than one object on the Stage and click on one or more of its buttons to align them.

◎◎ Applying Color

Up to this point, you've been learning how to draw in Flash with little regard to color. You can choose colors when drawing new objects, or change the colors of existing objects. There are several ways to select colors. (You might even think there are too many ways.) Choose the method that suits you.

Colors on the Tools Panel

Every object in Flash can have both a stroke and a fill. The stroke has its own color and so does the fill. From the Colors section of the Tools panel, click on the fill or stroke **swatch** (square of color) and a color grid will pop up (see Figure 2.8), allowing you to select a color. The selected color will apply to whichever tool (e.g., Brush, Pencil) is active. If an object has been selected, it will change to this color.

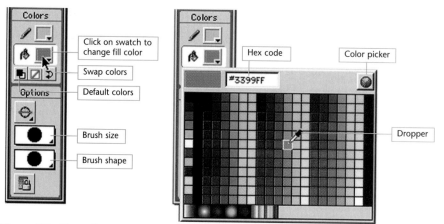

Figure 2.8   The color pop-up from the Tools panel.

The color grid in Flash includes Web-safe colors. These are a limited set of 216 colors that display more predictably on all Web browsers. Other colors may not look the same for everyone or may not display smoothly. If you decide you want to use another color anyway, click on the color picker icon to choose from a full spectrum of colors. See the *Web Wizard's Guide to HTML* or the Online References section at the end of the chapter for more information on Web-safe colors.

Trade the fill color with the stroke color by clicking on the **Swap Colors** arrow button. Or, reset the colors to black and white by clicking on the **Default Colors** button.

Color Panels

You can choose the same colors with the **Mixer** and **Swatches** panels as you would from the Tools panel, but with a few more options. (If the panels are not visible, open them from the Windows menu.) To specify colors from the Mixer pane, enter numeric values or click in the color bar rainbow. Select a color from the grid of color squares on the Swatches panel just as you would from the Tools panel.

Modify the stroke or fill of an object with their respective panels. Specify the thickness of a stroke, its style, and color in the **Stroke** panel. The **Fill** panel allows you to select colors from swatches, and it provides controls for gradient fills.

☆ **FLASH MX**   No More Stroke and Fill Panels

Flash MX does away with the Fill and Stroke panels. Instead, these settings are available from the Properties Inspector when an ungrouped object is selected (see bottom of Figure 2.9).

Once you find that perfect color, you can save it from the Mixer panel. Choose *Add Swatch* from that panel's Options menu. This will append the color to the bottom of the Swatches panel. Delete a selected swatch by choosing *Delete Swatch* from the Swatches panel's options.

Dropper Tool

After you have created an object, it is unlikely that you would remember its exact colors. Use the Dropper tool to select a color from any existing object on the Stage and it will apply it to whatever tool or object is selected.

Gradient Fills and Bitmap Fills

A **gradient** fill is a gradual change in tone or color. It can add dimension to your artwork when used appropriately. Since Flash is a vector application, you can use gradients for shading with little impact on file size.

☆ **FLASH MX**   Gradient Fills and Bitmap Fills in Flash MX

In Flash MX, the gradient and bitmap fill options are moved to the Mixer panel. Also, the Fill Transform tool replaces the Paint Bucket's Transform Fill option.

Apply a gradient fill as you would a solid color. Choose an existing gradient from the Swatches panel (see Figure 2.9) and click with the Paint Bucket tool to apply it to an object.

To create a new gradient, pull down the menu at the top of the Fill panel and select *Radial Gradient* or *Linear Gradient* (use the Mixer panel in Flash MX). To modify the gradient, move the sliders that appear and change their colors (see Figure 2.10). Apply the gradient once or save it for later from the Options menu on the Fill panel.

Applying Color

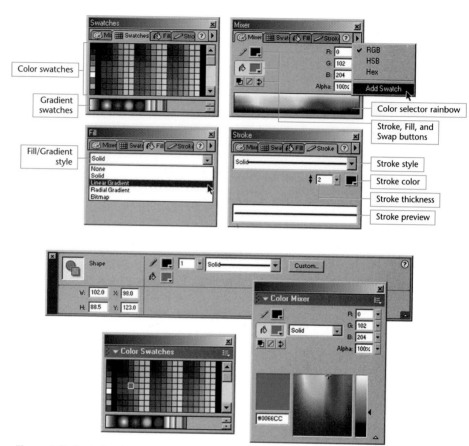

Figure 2.9 Flash 5 color panels (top). The Fill and Stroke panels are replaced by the Properties Inspector in Flash MX (bottom).

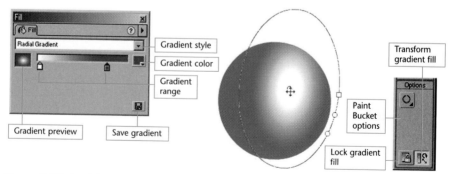

Figure 2.10 Applying a gradient fill with the Fill panel and Paint Bucket options.

To adjust the positioning and shape of a gradient, first choose the Paint Bucket tool and its Transform Fill option. Then select a gradient-filled object with the Paint Bucket and it will sprout controls for adjusting the position and shape of the gradient's shading (see Figure 2.10).

> ☆WARNING   **Don't Overuse Gradients**
>
> Gradient fills are kind to the file size of your files, but too many could clutter your design. Also, they affect how fast a computer displays a Flash movie.

If you have imported any bitmap images into your file (covered later in this chapter) you can choose one as a fill. Pull down the menu on the Fill panel and choose *Bitmap* (use the Mixer panel in Flash MX). Next, choose a bitmap image from that same panel. Like a gradient fill, you can reposition a bitmap fill with the Paint Bucket tool.

◎◉ Working with Multiple Objects

Once you have created an object in Flash, you can draw over it to change it. Any tool will do: Brush, Pen, or Oval. Use the same color to add to a shape; or use a different color and you'll create a second adjacent shape. You could also use copy (Edit→Copy) and paste (Edit→Paste) to duplicate a selected object.

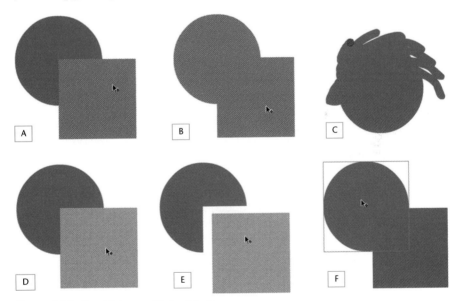

Figure 2.11 Combining multiple objects.

☆ Place a new object over a same-color object and they merge into a single shape (see Figure 2.11, A and B).

☆ Add to a shape with the Brush tool (see Figure 2.11, C).

☆ Place a shape of a different color and it will cut into the other shape (see Figure 2.11, D and E).

If you want to keep selected objects separate, you can choose Modify→Group to create a **Group** (see Figure 2.11, F). Grouped objects are autonomous and will not mix with other objects. You can reposition, scale, or rotate groups like other objects, but they will always stay separate. Choose Modify→Ungroup or Modify→Break Apart to ungroup objects. However, you will be learning about layers and symbols which are better for separating or grouping objects.

◎◎ Utilizing Layers

Layers work like overlays and are an important organizational tool in Flash. They are based on the concept of overlays in classic graphic design. Overlays are clear sheets of plastic laid one over another. Each sheet contains a graphic object, allowing other layers below to show through outside of that object.

If you have used another graphics program, such as Photoshop or Freehand, you may be familiar with layers. You can create one layer for an imported bitmap image and another for a cartoon character that's placed in front of that image. Insert another layer for some text, another for some more text, and one more for a different character. In the coming chapters, you will add layers to create animation or other effects.

Here are a few reasons for adding layers:

☆ To be sure that one object appears in front of another.

☆ To distinguish different elements on the Stage.

☆ To animate a specific object on the Stage.

☆ To prevent one graphic object from merging with or cutting into another.

☆ To organize elements for easier editing.

☆ To separate frame actions, labels, or sound from the other elements in the movie.

Adding and Deleting Layers

Layers are managed in the Timeline. The left side lists the layer names with the corresponding frames to the right (see Figure 1.6). Each layer on the Timeline corresponds to a layer that appears on the Stage. The contents of layers at the top of the list appear in front of the layers lower on the list.

Choose Insert→Layer to add a layer to the current Timeline. Conveniently, below the layer names are a few buttons for adding and removing layers. Click on the first button to add a layer. The second button adds guide layers (covered in Chapter Three); and the trash can symbol deletes selected layers (see Figure 2.12). Right-click (Ctrl-click for Macintosh) on any layer name to reveal a contextual menu for adding, deleting, or editing layers.

Create as many layers as you like. There's no limit, but the more layers you create, the more you will have to manage as you edit the Flash file. Some people add layers liberally and others are more frugal. Over time, you will get a feeling for how many layers are right for you.

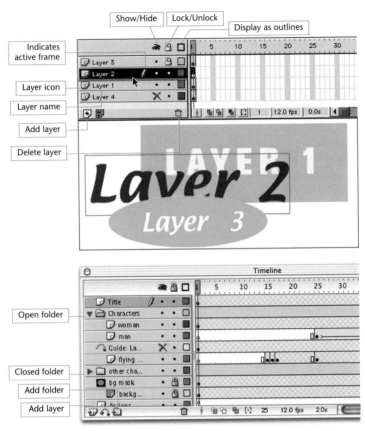

Figure 2.12 Layers appear on the Stage but are organized from the Timeline (top). The Flash MX Timeline (bottom) offers folders to group sets of layers.

Organizing Layers

By default, Flash names new layers with numbers: (Layer 1, Layer 2, Layer 3). If you are only using two or three layers, those names will work fine. When you create more layers than that, descriptive names will help you to identify their contents (e.g., Barking Dog, House, Moving Cloud, Main Headline, Actions, Play Button). To rename a layer, first double-click on the current name to select it, and then type in the new name.

The order of the layers determines what appears on top or behind. The *top layer* in the Timeline will appear as the *top layer* on the Stage. Figure 2.12 should help you visualize this. To change the order of a layer, click and drag it up or down on the list.

☆ **FLASH MX   Layer Folders**

Flash MX introduces layer folders. Add a layer folder to the Timeline as you would a standard layer. Add other layers to it by dragging their names over the folder. You cannot add frames to layer folders, just other layers.

Utilizing Layers

Displaying and Locking Layers

Click the icons just to the right of each layer name (see Figure 2.12) to change the display of the layers while you are working in Flash. [Alt]-click on an icon ([Option]-click for Macintosh) and the option will be applied to every layer *except* the one you are clicking on. These settings do not affect which layers are published.

☆ Show/Hide: Hide a layer to uncover the layers beneath it. Click it again to reveal the layer again.

☆ Unlock/Lock: Lock a layer and it's still visible, but you can't inadvertently move or edit anything in it. When you want to edit a locked layer, click the icon to unlock it.

☆ Layers as Outlines: Display the objects in a layer as outlines to speed the display. Click it again to return to a normal display.

☆ **FLASH MX   Distribute to Layers**

If you've got more than one object on a single layer and you want to move any of them to other layers, there's a new command in Flash MX. Select whatever objects you want to move and then choose the Modify→Distribute to Layers. This will create a new layer for each selected object and place it there.

◎◎ Importing Bitmap Images

By now, you should know the virtues of vector graphics, but sometimes only a bitmap image will do. Maybe it's a scanned photograph or some clip art. Or maybe you want the qualities of a bitmap illustration created in a program such as Adobe Photoshop or Fractal Design Painter. Flash accepts several different formats of bitmap files.

Assuming that you have first saved an image in another program, choose File→Import and a dialog box will pop up. Navigate through that window until you locate and select the desired image file. Then click the *Open* button and the desired image will appear on the Stage. (In the Macintosh version of Flash 5, click the *Add* button, then the *Import* button.) To import artwork, an unlocked layer must be active. Upon import, the artwork will be placed on the Stage in the active layer. You can resize, rotate, or move a bitmap image as you would any other object on the Stage. If you choose Modify→Break Apart, you will be able to select, remove, or recolor any part of the bitmap image.

Saving Bitmap Files in Other Programs

If you have never worked with bitmap images or saved them for the Web, you should consult a book such as *The Web Wizard's Guide to Multimedia*. Here is a quick overview of how to prepare images for use in Flash.

While you are working in a bitmap program, you usually will have a choice of formats for saving the artwork. Flash recognizes several popular graphic formats, but you'll get the best results if you can save the images in either GIF or JPEG format. If you optimize a GIF or JPEG image in another program, Flash will preserve its settings.

Chapter Six addresses optimizing bitmap images once you are working in Flash. When saving images in a bitmap program, a general rule of thumb is to save scanned photographs or drawings as JPEG images and graphic artwork as GIFs. Macromedia Fireworks and Adobe ImageReady are the best programs for saving images in these formats.

If you aren't satisfied with the image quality of the JPEG or GIF format, try PNG. You can use the PNG format for irregular shapes—it will preserve transparent parts of an object (see Figure 2.13). The file size of PNG images can be larger than GIF or JPEG files, so use this format only when you need it.

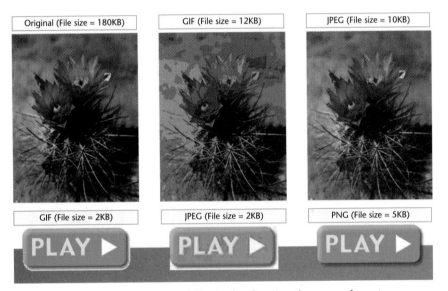

Figure 2.13 Maximize the quality and file size by choosing the proper format.

☆ SHORTCUT   **Copy and Paste:**
The Simplest Way to Import Artwork

You don't have to rely on the import command. Chances are, you can directly copy an object from the open window of one graphics program, such as Photoshop or Freehand, and paste it onto the Flash stage. In the Macintosh version of Flash, you can drag the icon of an image file (or sound file) directly from your computer's desktop onto the Stage.

Look at Figure 2.13. Notice the difference in quality between the GIF and JPEG formats of the photograph. Not only does the GIF format distort the photograph but it also adds more to the file size than the JPEG image.

The PLAY button uses flat colors and text, so it works better as a GIF image. You could save it as a JPEG, but it wouldn't be as sharp. Saving it as a PNG image results in the best overall quality and allows its shadow to be transparent and blend with the background, but the file size is larger.

Convert Bitmap to Vector

Maybe you want to apply vector attributes to a bitmap image. After you have imported a bitmap image into Flash, you can convert it to a vector image. Keep in mind that this is no replacement for creating vector artwork in the first place, and it won't work well for every image. You'll have to try it out on different images to see how it works.

This command will only work if you have not already used Modify→Break Apart. With a bitmap image selected on the Stage, choose Modify→Trace Bitmap to convert it to a vector image. A window will pop up with various settings. You can experiment with different values here. Depending on the image, this may help improve file size and the appearance of artwork; you may also use it to create a special effect.

◎◎ Working with Other Vector Programs

The Flash drawing tools are good for the basics, but if you're creating something more complex, a vector-based illustration program such as Adobe Illustrator or Macromedia Freehand may work better. Or maybe you're working with an artist who prefers to use one of those programs. Flash can import artwork seamlessly from Illustrator, Freehand, or even Macromedia Fireworks. And once it's in Flash, you can edit artwork as you would any other objects you'd create directly in Flash. In most cases, you can edit the text as well.

When you import artwork into Flash, it comes grouped, which prevents you from fully editing it. If you don't need to change anything but its position or size, you can leave it grouped. If you want to change the shape, color, or text, ungroup it first. Choose Ungroup from the Modify menu. In some cases, you may have to do this more than once and apply the Modify→Break Apart command.

Macromedia Freehand

Since Macromedia makes both products, they designed Freehand to work optimally with Flash, and vice versa. In fact, you can get a discount if you purchase both programs together. With Freehand you can create a simple drawing or construct a complete animation.

This program shares other features of Flash besides vector graphics, and version 10 includes the Controller toolbar, which is dedicated for previewing and exporting Flash files. Freehand uses layers and symbols which translate into Flash. You can even create animations with it.

If you want to see how this works, download "Freehand Animation" for Chapter Two from the Flash section at http://www.aw.com/webwizard. Import the saved file into a new Flash file. Once it's open, hit the [Enter] key on your keyboard to see a Flash animation created in Freehand.

From Freehand, export a Flash SWF file by choosing File→Export. Choose *Macromedia Flash (SWF)* as the format. If you want to modify the way the file will export, click on the *Setup* button before the *Export* button. After it is saved, import that SWF file into Flash from File→Import.

Adobe Illustrator

If you own Illustrator and are comfortable with it, you probably won't miss Freehand. Illustrator 9 offers good support for Flash and Illustrator 10 offers even more. To export Illustrator artwork to Flash, choose File→Export in Illustrator, and a Save window will pop up. From that window, choose *Flash (SWF)* from the Format menu and click the *Export* button. Next, you will see a window with Flash-specific settings. You can leave them alone or change them before clicking *OK*.

Macromedia Fireworks

Fireworks is an unique program. It's a hybrid vector and bitmap program. Fireworks was designed specifically for creating GIF and JPEG images for Web pages, but it can also create Flash SWF files. With Fireworks you can compose a bitmap graphic, a vector graphic, or a mix of both. To save a file for Flash, choose File→Export. Next, choose *Macromedia SWF* from the Save As menu before clicking the *Save* button. Like Freehand, you can click the *Options* button before saving.

☆ **WARNING**   **Some Vector Effects Will Not Import**

Most of what you create in other vector programs will import seamlessly into Flash. However, if you've used a more advanced feature in any of these programs, such as mesh gradient, pattern fills, or certain special effects, they may not translate into Flash. Sometimes the file will be completely unusable, and other times you'll get all the art and type minus a few special effects. The latest versions of Freehand, Illustrator, and Fireworks allow you to export your artwork in the Flash SWF format. This is a more reliable way to translate it to Flash.

◎◎ Using Text in Flash

You can use text for just one word on a logo or for several paragraphs. Flash can create text that's much richer than what appears on a standard HTML Web page. Flash does not limit you to the fonts (typefaces) your audience has available on their computers; you can use any font from your own computer while building the movie. Standard HTML doesn't provide a way to size and space text exactly as you want, but Flash does.

Adding Text to the Stage

To add or edit text in a Flash movie, choose the Text tool from the Tools panel. Click it on the Stage, then type from the keyboard, and you will see what you type right on the Stage (see Figure 2.14). Click down, drag, and release with the Text tool to automatically constrain the text to a specific width. Otherwise the text will continue in a straight line until you hit the [Return] key on your keyboard. When you have finished typing, you will have created a text block.

Rather than typing in Flash, you can place text in Flash from your favorite word processing program. First, select and copy the text from your word processing document. Then switch to your Flash document. Click (or click and drag) on the Stage with the Text tool to define a text area, and then paste the text (Edit→Paste).

Formatting Text

With the Text tool, you can select individual words or characters in a text block and use the Text panels to change color, spacing, or fonts. With the Arrow tool, you can select an entire text block to move, resize, or rotate it.

☆ **FLASH MX** **Text Settings Move to the Properties Inspector**

Flash MX has no text panels. When you select text or create a text box, all of the same options are now available from the Properties Inspector panel.

Figure 2.14 The text panels in Flash 5 (top). The text settings are available from the Properties Inspector in Flash MX (bottom).

Character

The Character panel applies to whatever text is selected, whether it is just one character or several paragraphs. You can change the font to whatever is available on your computer and make it big or small. Use the *Kern* and *Tracking* options to change the way the individual characters are spaced. You can change the color of the text here as well. The text color is the same as the fill color in Flash, so you can change the fill color on any panel to affect the selected text.

Create a link to any Web page with the URL option. Type the address of a Web site in the URL box (e.g., `http://www.yahoo.com`) and your audience will be able to click on the selected text to go to another Web page.

Paragraph

The Paragraph panel settings affect entire paragraphs. Click on one of the Align buttons to change the alignment of the text. At the bottom of the panel you can change the indents of the text as well as the space between lines.

Text Options

This panel is for more advanced dynamic text features. There are three options here: *Static Text*, *Dynamic Text*, and *Input Text*. Use Static Text unless you need to implement dynamic behavior or user input boxes. (Consult an ActionScript reference for using the other modes.) There are two options in the Static Text mode:

☆ *Use Device Fonts* slightly cuts the file size of your final SWF file by not including fonts. When this option is checked, your audience might not see the movie in the same fonts as you do and the savings is not very great. It's better to leave it unchecked unless you really need the savings.

☆ The *Selectable* option allows your audience to select the text in their Web browsers. This is a good idea for longer passages of text because it allows users to copy it and save it elsewhere for reference.

Converting Text into Standard Vector Objects

Choose Modify→Break Apart to convert a text block into vector objects that can be reshaped, painted, and modified just like other Flash objects. However, once you do this, you will not be able to edit it as text again.

☆ **FLASH MX   Changed Behavior for Breaking Apart Text**

In Flash MX, the Break Apart command preserves text as text objects, but each character becomes a separate text object. If you want to convert text to a plain graphic object, use this command a second time on the separated characters.

☆ Summary

▷ Use the File menu to create, save, and open Flash files.

▷ To draw in Flash, use the Pencil, Brush, or Pen tool from the Tools panel; or choose the Oval or Rectangle tool to draw simple shapes.

▷ Select an object with the Arrow tool, and then move or transform it.

▷ Change the fill or stroke color of an object directly from the Tools panel, or access more options from one of the color panels.

▷ You don't need to work exclusively in Flash. Import bitmap or vector artwork from other programs as is, or alter it with the Flash tools.

▷ Create or edit text with the Text tool and format it with the Character and Paragraph panels.

☆ Online References

Web-Safe Colors
`http://www.lynda.com/hex.html`

Using the Flash 5 Pen Tool
`http://www.flash411.com/f5_presentation/f5_illustration.html`

GIF versus JPEG Bitmap Compression
`http://coe.sdsu.edu/eet/Articles/wpdgifjpg/start.htm`

Optimizing Bitmap Images
`http://www.webmonkey.com/99/15/index0a.html`

Adobe ImageReady and Photoshop
`http://www.adobe.com/products/photoshop/`

Exporting SWF files from Freehand and Fireworks
`http://www.macromedia.com/support/general/ts/documents/fw_fh_swf.htm`

Using Freehand to Create Flash Files
`http://www.elementkjournals.com/freehand/article7/article7.htm`

Using Illustrator with Flash
`http://www.adobe.com/products/illustrator/keyfeature1.html`

Flash Typography Tips
`http://builder.cnet.com/webbuilding/pages/Graphics/`
`FlashPoint/062600/ss02.html`
Loading HTML Text into a Flash Movie
`http://www.macromedia.com/support/flash/ts/documents/`
`htmltext.htm`

☆ Review Questions

1. Where do you change the frame rate of a Flash movie?

2. What is the preferred unit of measurement for Flash and other Web-based projects?

3. Which drawing tool creates just fill shapes? Which tool do you use to add a stroke to a fill shape?

4. Which tools are the easiest to use for creating a simple circular or rectangular shape? Which key on the keyboard helps you to draw a perfect square?

5. Which tool is the most popular for selecting an object on the Stage? How do you remove an object?

6. How do you enlarge or rotate an object?

7. Name two panels that you can use to change a color.

8. When exporting a file in Adobe Illustrator, which format translates most reliably into Flash? Which format works best with scanned photographs?

9. How do you convert text into a standard vector object?

10. Describe one way to place a bitmap image into a Flash movie.

☆ Hands-On Exercises

1. Find an actual physical ruler (plastic, metal, or wood). Create a new Flash document and set the ruler units to centimeters or inches. Hold the ruler up to your computer display and compare the measurements of the physical ruler to the Flash ruler. (If the rulers aren't visible, choose View→Rulers.) Change the magnification of the Flash movie with the Zoom tool and compare the rulers again. Draw a rectangle and measure it with the physical ruler. Then select the rectangle and note the values in the Info panel. Describe your observations.

2. a. Create a new Flash document. Set the dimensions to 400 pixels wide by 300 pixels high. Change the background color of your movie to a light blue. Draw a perfect circle on the stage. Make the fill of the circle orange and its stroke red.

   b. Use the Pencil tool to draw one shape with the smooth modifier and one with the straighten modifier. Use the Arrow tool to make the first line smoother and the second line straighter.

    c. Use the Brush tool to draw an object. Reshape it with the Arrow tool.

    d. Save the file.

3. Draw two rectangles that intersect the circle from the first exercise: one rectangle with the same fill color, and one with a different fill color. Use the Arrow tool (the Free Transform tool for Flash MX) to reshape the objects, and then enlarge them. Save the file.

4. Add a new layer to the same Flash document. From the Web Wizard Web site, download the "Chapter Two Exercises" link. Add a layer and import the Freehand file *flower.fh9* into the Flash movie. Change the colors and shape of the flower. Rotate it exactly 60 degrees. Make a few duplicates of this flower and arrange them on the Stage. Add another layer and import the file named *background.jpg*. Enlarge it to fill the Stage. Arrange it so that it appears behind everything else in the movie. Save the file.

5. Type a headline onto the Flash Stage. Make the size of the headline 36 points in any font you like. Below that, type a paragraph of smaller text in Arial. Make the smaller text selectable (and legible). All of this text should appear in front of everything else. Save the file.

CHAPTER THREE

FLASH ANIMATION

Animation is the bread and butter of Flash. Now that you've read through Chapter Two, you should be familiar with creating and importing artwork. So far, these objects have just been sitting motionless on the Stage. This chapter explains how to bring them to life. You'll be learning how to add **symbols** to your Flash movie, and how to use **keyframes** and **tweening** to control animation.

Chapter Objectives

☆ Get familiar with the Timeline

☆ Add and manipulate frames and keyframes

☆ Create and edit symbols

☆ Construct three types of animation

☆ Use animation for non-motion effects

☆ Utilize onion skinning, guide layers, and masks

☆ Manage symbols and other assets in the library

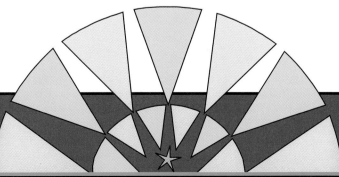

◎◎ Working with Frames in the Timeline

To create animation, something must change over time. An object can move, spin, change color, grow, or disappear. While these changes appear on the Stage, the Timeline controls *when* they change. The Timeline navigates to different views on the Stage.

Keyframes Create Change

Flash uses **keyframes** to designate change, or to create animation. When you start with a new movie, there is only one frame, a keyframe (see Figure 1.6, top). A keyframe denotes a single view on the Stage. As you'll see later in this book, keyframes are also the place where you specify attributes such as animation tweening, scripting, and sounds.

To edit a keyframe, you use the Timeline *and* the Stage. Every time you want something to change in a Flash movie, you first add a keyframe to the Timeline. To add a keyframe to the movie, click somewhere in the Timeline and choose the Insert→Keyframe command. This will add a keyframe wherever you click.

When you add a keyframe, you create a new view for the Stage. The Stage will change when the playhead on the Timeline moves from one keyframe to the next. If you move an object, add something new, or take something away between the first keyframe and the new keyframe, you create animation.

Standard Frames Add Time

All frames on the Timeline add time to the play of a movie. Keyframes add time, but are best used when you also want to designate a change. Use standard frames when all you need to add is time. Standard frames fill the space between keyframes.

To extend the play of a movie, add standard frames between or after keyframes. Wherever you click on the Timeline, the Insert→Frame command will add a new standard frame at that point.

☆ If you click and drag to select a range of frames, Flash will insert the same number of new frames that were selected.

☆ Click somewhere past the last frame on the Timeline and insert a frame to extend the movie to that point.

☆ [Shift]-click to highlight frames in multiple layers and insert frames to all of them all at once.

☆ **SHORTCUT**   **Frame Shortcuts**

Right-click ([Ctrl]-click for Macintosh) anywhere in the Timeline to pop up a contextual menu for the Timeline. You can add or remove frames from this menu. The [F5] key is handy for adding frames. Select a frame in the Timeline and hit it 20 times and you've added 20 frames. The [F6] key will insert a keyframe.

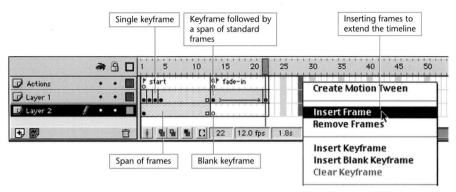

Figure 3.1 The Timeline with a few keyframes and layers.

Identifying Frames

One keyframe can follow another keyframe, or it can mark the beginning of a span (or block) of frames. Look at Figure 3.1. There are several ways to visually identify frames in the Timeline:

☆ A dot signifies a keyframe and a black line outlines the span of frames that follow it.

☆ A solid black dot inside a shaded block indicates that there is an object in the keyframe.

☆ If there is no shading or no black dot, there is no object in the keyframe. A hollow circle indicates a blank keyframe.

☆ There are light gray hash marks where there are no frames.

The look of the frames and the way you select them can be changed in the Preferences (Edit→Preferences). The *Flash 4 Selection Style* and *Flash 4 Frame Drawing* options make keyframes easier to select and identify. The instructions in this book assume that both options are checked.

Moving and Duplicating Frames

It's inevitable: You will move frames as you work. You may want to change the design of your movie, you may need to tweak an animation, or you may choose to reorder some content.

Moving frames is fairly straightforward. Click on a frame to select it. Then drag the selection to a new position in the Timeline. Here are a few other techniques:

☆ Click and drag to select a range of frames.

☆ Shift-click to add to a selection.

☆ Ctrl-click (⌘-click for Macintosh) to select nonconsecutive frames.

☆ Hold down the Alt key (Option key for Macintosh) on your keyboard. Then drag a selection to duplicate it.

Right-click ([Ctrl]-click for Macintosh) to reveal options to copy, cut, paste, or remove selected frames. (These commands are also available under the Edit and Insert menus.) You can create an animation in one part of the Timeline, copy or cut it, and then paste it somewhere else. *Clear Keyframe* will convert a selected keyframe into a standard frame.

☆ **FLASH MX**   **Improved Frame Handling**

Selecting, moving, and duplicating frames is more intuitive in Flash MX than in earlier versions. For example, you now can double-click to select a span of frames. The same techniques described above work as well.

☆ **SHORTCUT**   **Moving Objects with Paste in Place**

There are times when all the frames and keyframes are in the right place on the Timeline, but their contents on the Stage need to be moved between keyframes. In this case, it's better to leave the Timeline alone and move the objects directly from the Stage.

The Copy or Cut command under the Edit menu stores selected objects in a hidden clipboard file. Edit→Paste will place a copy of those contents in the center of the Stage. If you're moving objects from the Stage in one keyframe to the Stage in another keyframe, you'd have to reposition them after this. Edit→Paste in Place does the same thing as Edit→Paste, but places the objects in the same position as they were when copied.

◎◎ Creating Frame-by-Frame Animation

Adding an additional keyframe allows you to create animation. You can create a separate keyframe and reposition artwork on the Stage for each tick of the Timeline. This is called **frame-by-frame animation**.

First, create a two-frame animation:

☆ Start by drawing something in the first keyframe.

☆ Add a second keyframe just after the first, and on the same layer (Insert→Keyframe). When you add a new keyframe, it inherits any objects that existed on a previous keyframe. (If you don't want that to happen, choose Insert→Blank Keyframe instead.)

☆ From the Stage, move the drawing in the second keyframe to a different position from where it is in the first keyframe. Between keyframes, an object can change position, shape, color, size, or disappear. That's animation.

Once you have tried these steps, hit the [Enter] key on your keyboard to see it play. A two-frame animation may not be as impressive as a feature cartoon, but it is animation all the same. Add several more keyframes, one after another, to build the animation however you like. This is frame-by-frame animation (see Figure 3.2).

Look for an example of frame-by-frame animation and other techniques explained throughout this book on the Web Wizard Web site: http://www.aw.com/webwizard.

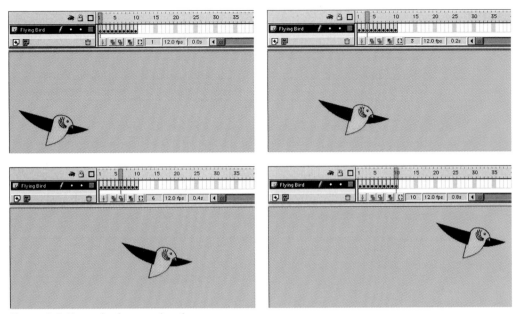

Figure 3.2 Frame-by-frame animation.

◎◎ Introducing Symbols

As your Flash movie grows in complexity, creating separate objects for each keyframe is not very efficient. It's tedious work and doesn't help you keep the file size small. And if you copy the same object a dozen times and later want to change its color, you'd have to change the color a dozen times. Flash symbols provide the alternative to this work.

A **symbol instance** appears the same as the original symbol, but it is not a complete copy of it. It is a reference to the original symbol in the library. Any object on the Stage can be converted to a symbol. A symbol is stored in the **library**, and you place one or more instances of a symbol on the Stage. Generally, you should create a symbol for anything that appears more than once in a movie. Soon you will learn how to apply symbols to a motion tween animation, and in Chapter Four you'll apply them to actions.

After it's placed on the Stage, you can alter the position, size, or rotation of an individual symbol instance, or apply an effect to it. This will not affect the original symbol or any other instances of it. However, if you make changes to the original symbol, every instance will be updated.

This is useful if you are collaborating with an illustrator. You could set up the symbol with a rough sketch as a placeholder. Place instances of that symbol throughout the movie, and when the final artwork is ready, you'd just edit the original symbol. You wouldn't have to touch a single instance to update all of them (See Figure 6.1.).

How to Create a Symbol

You can create symbols in one of two ways:

 Convert selected art to a symbol: Create some artwork on the Stage, select it, and choose the Insert→Convert to Symbol command. In Flash 5, this is the quickest way to create a symbol. It leaves an instance of the new symbol on the Stage and saves it for you in the library.

 Create a new symbol from scratch: Choose the Insert→New Symbol command and you will go to a blank Stage and Timeline, where you can begin composing the symbol. There, you can draw, import art, or do anything else that you would on the movie's main Stage and Timeline.

> ☆ **FLASH MX**   **New Ways to Convert to Symbol**
>
> In Flash MX, you can drag an object from the Stage to the library to convert it to a Symbol. Or, right-click ([Ctrl]-click for Macintosh) on an object and choose *Convert to Symbol* from the contextual menu that pops up.

Symbol Behavior

Whenever you create a symbol, the **Symbol Properties** box will pop up (see Figure 3.3). From that box you can name the symbol and choose its **Behavior**. This has no bearing on what a symbol looks like, but directs how it behaves on the Stage of the movie. You can later change an existing symbol's behavior from the library or override it for a single instance from the Instance panel. There are three types of symbol behavior.

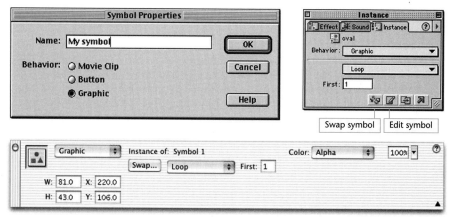

Figure 3.3 Symbol Properties and the Instance panel (top). In Flash MX, the instance settings are moved to the Properties Inspector (bottom).

Graphic Behavior

A **graphic** symbol is the most basic type. If you're not sure about which type of symbol you are creating, choose *Graphic* behavior. This is the type of symbol you'll be creating in this chapter. It's the best choice for a static, non-moving object. If you want, you can also add layers, frames, sounds, and other symbol instances to a graphic symbol as you would the main movie.

Button Behavior

The **button** symbol is the most specific type of symbol. It has built-in behaviors that allow it to respond visually to the mouse. Chapter Four explains the button symbol and discusses how to apply actions to it. Actions allow a user to change the way a movie plays when a button is clicked: to stop it, start it, or move to somewhere else.

Movie Clip Behavior

A **movie clip** symbol is a lot like a graphic symbol. It is the usual choice for an animated symbol, such as a spinning ball. A movie clip instance can also be named and controlled with actions, as you'll learn in Chapter Four.

Editing Symbols

Like a mini-Flash movie, each symbol has its own Stage and Timeline. You can add layers, frames, and actions to a symbol just like you would in the main Flash movie. The button symbol has one exception: It has only four frames (see Chapter Four). Whenever you create a new symbol (Insert→New Symbol) or edit an existing one, you will be presented with a separate Stage and Timeline to work on. This is the symbol-editing mode.

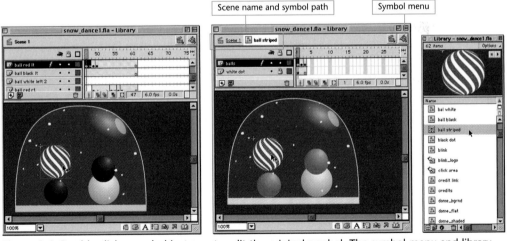

Figure 3.4 Double-click a symbol instance to edit the original symbol. The symbol menu and library also access symbols for editing.

On the Stage, double-click on any symbol instance to edit the corresponding symbol (see Figure 3.4). You will see the rest of the Stage area ghosted, or faded. The symbol's name appears above the Timeline or Stage. This is the symbol path to let you know what you are editing. When you want to return to the Stage, double-click outside of the symbol.

Here are a few other ways to edit a symbol:

☆ Right-click on a symbol instance ([Ctrl]-click for Macintosh) and choose *Edit In Place* or *Edit In New Window* from the contextual pop-up menu.

☆ Double-click a symbol in the library to edit it on the Stage.

☆ Choose the symbol name from the symbol pull-down menu in the upper right corner above the Stage.

To return to the main Timeline when you are finished editing a symbol, choose the Edit→Edit Movie command ([Ctrl]-[E] for Windows, [⌘]-[E] for Macintosh).

☆ **SHORTCUT   Swapping Symbols**

There are times when you have positioned a symbol instance in a particular place and possibly even applied transformations, but you decide to use a new or different symbol. All you need to do is link the instance to a different symbol in the library. With a symbol instance selected, click the Swap button at the bottom of the instance panel (see Figure 3.3). In Flash MX, the Swap button is available on the Properties Inspector panel.

◉◎ Animating with a Motion Tween

Frame-by-frame animation is a manual process. You add keyframe after keyframe, moving the objects by hand each time. You need many keyframes, a steady eye, and a lot of patience to create smooth motion. A motion tween can do the same thing automatically using only two keyframes.

Keyframes and *tweening* are terms from classic animation, before there were personal computers. In traditional animation, a master animator draws the *key frames*, which are key points in the animation. The master animator gives the *key frame* drawings to an in-be*tween* artist with specific instructions. The in-be*tween* artist has the laborious task of drawing the many frames that belong between the *key frames*.

With Flash, you are the master animator and Flash supplies the in-be*tween* artist. Set up two keyframes that surround a range of standard frames, add a motion tween, and Flash calculates what happens between. It's the most efficient way to create motion in Flash.

How to Create a Motion Tween

To create a motion tween, it's best to add a separate layer first. A motion tween allows you to animate only one object at a time. On this layer, you will isolate a single symbol instance to animate.

☆ After adding a new layer, you'll need a symbol to animate. With the first keyframe of the new layer active, draw something on the Stage. Use the Insert→Convert to Symbol command to convert it to a symbol. Name the symbol and choose *Graphic* as the behavior.

☆ In the same layer, insert a second keyframe, several frames (10–20) past the first keyframe (see Figure 3.5, A). This will automatically duplicate the symbol instance in the same position.

☆ Remember, to create animation, something must change between the frames. Use the Arrow tool to drag the symbol instance on the Stage in the second keyframe to a different position (see Figure 3.5, B). You can adjust the position of the instance in the first keyframe as well.

☆ In the Timeline, select the first keyframe. The quickest way to do this is to click on that keyframe on the Timeline.

☆ With the first keyframe selected, go to the Frame panel (Properties Inspector in Flash MX) and choose *Motion* from the Tweening menu there (see Figure 3.5, C). You don't need to change any of the other tween options to make a symbol move.

That's a motion tween. It automatically applies the differences in position incrementally, to however many standard frames there are between the two keyframes. When played, you will see a gradual motion (see Figure 3.5, D).

The more frames there are between the two keyframes, the smoother the motion will be and the more time it will take. If you want to extend the animation in a different direction, add another keyframe and another motion tween just after the first one.

☆ **FLASH MX   Goodbye to the Frame, Instance, and Effect Panels**

When you select a frame or a symbol instance in Flash MX, the corresponding options will be available in the Properties Inspector.

☆ **WARNING   One Symbol Instance Per Tween, Please**

A motion tween allows just a single symbol instance for each keyframe. Also, both the start and end keyframe must contain an instance of exactly the same symbol. If you add more objects to either keyframe, the Flash player won't know what to tween. To animate a second object, add a second layer.

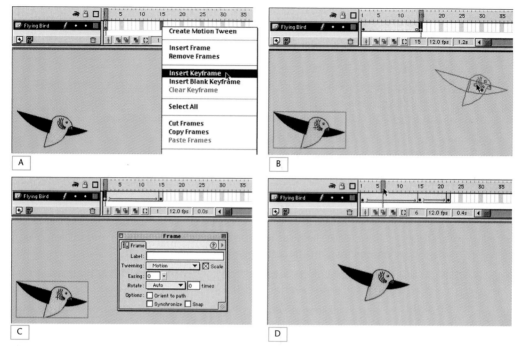

Figure 3.5 Creating motion tween animation.

Checking a Motion Tween

The Timeline is your best clue as to whether a motion tween is set up correctly. Wherever there is a motion tween, the tweened frames are shaded blue (green for shape tweens). An arrow between the two keyframes indicates that one frame is tweening to the next.

If you see a dashed line, something is amiss (see Figure 3.6). Make sure that you have an instance of exactly the same symbol in both keyframes and that they are on the same layer. Also be sure that there are no extraneous objects or symbols on either keyframe, just a single instance of the same symbol.

Playing the Animation

As you work through a Flash project, you should check your work often. To see how an animation progresses, play it. When you play a motion tween animation, the symbol should move evenly from one position to another.

Enter Key

If you hit the Enter key on your keyboard, the animation will play from whichever frame is active through the end of the movie. After the movie stops, hit the Enter key a second time to play it again from the beginning.

Animating with a Motion Tween

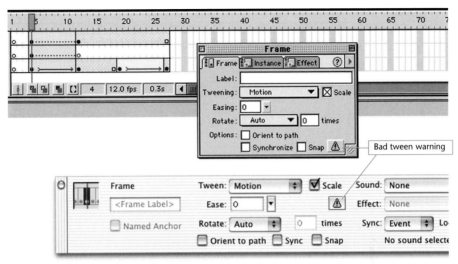

Figure 3.6 A dashed line in the Timeline indicates that something is wrong with a tween.

Playhead

The red frame indicator (the playhead) points to whichever frame is active on the Stage. Drag the indicator back and forth to change the active frame. This is less smooth than playing the animation, but it's a quick way to check how individual frames progress.

Controller

This is probably the most cumbersome method, with buttons like those on a VCR that control the animation. Choose Window→Controller to reveal the Controller window. Play the movie, rewind it, or step frame by frame.

Control Menu

The Control menu offers the same options as the Controller, but it also lists a few keyboard shortcuts.

Test Movie

This is the most accurate way to test the movie since it plays a SWF file like what you would publish to the Web. However, it launches the movie in a new window so it is more disruptive to your work. Use this option as you work, but not for every minute step of the way. Chapter Six goes into detail about this method.

◎◎ Creating Animated Symbols

Each symbol has its own Stage and Timeline. Like the main Flash movie, you can create animation there too. Whether it's frame-by frame animation or motion tween animation, a symbol instance can play like a miniature movie within the main movie.

You'll usually create symbol animation with a movie clip symbol (see the earlier section on symbol behavior). By default, the movie clip will play over and over again, independent of the main Timeline of the movie. This is called *looping*. If you create a movie clip of a spinning globe and place it on the Stage, it will spin again and again, even if the rest of the movie sits still. However, the frame rate of the movie clip is still determined by the setting for the overall movie (e.g., 12fps).

Create the animation within the movie clip as you would on the main Timeline of the movie. In fact, forget about the rest of the movie and approach the symbol as if you are editing a separate movie. Check how it loops so that the last frame flows naturally back to the first frame. Drag an instance of that symbol onto the Stage of the main movie and position it as you would any other symbol instance.

In some cases you may want a symbol's animation to stop with the main Timeline. You could create a symbol of a dog with moving legs. In this case, you may want the dog's legs to stop with the action in the main movie. A graphic symbol plays in synch with the main Timeline. If the movie stops, so does the animation in the graphic symbol. When placing a graphic symbol animation on the Stage, be sure that the Loop option is selected in the Instance panel (Properties Inspector for Flash MX).

☆WARNING   **Previewing Movie Clip Animations**

After you place a movie clip symbol on the Stage of a movie, it will be visible, but you won't be able to see it animate there. Use the Control→Test Movie command to preview it correctly.

◎◎ Nesting Symbols

A symbol can contain anything that the main movie has, even instances of other symbols. This is a common strategy as you use Flash to build more complicated objects. A button could contain a movie clip; or a movie clip symbol could contain several instances of a graphic symbol. Within a symbol of a dog, for example, the legs could be separate instances of another symbol.

When any symbol instance is contained by another symbol, it is called **nesting**. The containing symbol becomes the **parent** and each instance it contains is a **child**. While editing one symbol (the parent symbol), drag another symbol's instance from the library and it becomes the first symbol's child. Select an object on the Stage of the parent symbol and convert that object into a symbol, which becomes its child.

While editing nested symbols, you will probably lose track of which symbol is nested where. Double-click on a parent symbol until you find all of its children and grandkids. The order of nesting is displayed to the left active symbol in the symbol path above the Stage (see Figure 3.7).

Figure 3.7 Nested symbols.

◎◎ Motion Tween Is Not Just for Motion

In Flash, a motion tween doesn't have to move. The symbol can fade in or out, or change size or color. You can tween any change made to a symbol instance: position, size, rotation, color, transparency.

To show change, a motion tween requires two successive keyframes with an instance of the same symbol. The second instance should be different somehow from the first. In the previous section, that difference was *position*, which creates motion. Other properties can be changed to create different effects.

Modifying a Symbol Instance

When you first place a symbol instance on the Stage, it looks exactly like the original symbol. Each instance has properties that can be modified independently from the original symbol.

Transform an Instance

In the previous section, you learned how to create motion by changing the position of the instance in the second keyframe. You can make the symbol appear to grow or shrink by resizing the second instance. Scale or rotate a symbol instance just as you would any other object or group in Flash. Use the Arrow tool options (the Free Transform tool for Flash MX), or apply a *Transform* option under the Modify menu. You can even combine multiple transformations for other effects.

The Effect Panel

While a symbol instance is selected, you can change one of several properties with the **Effect** panel (see Figure 3.8).

☆ **Brightness** adjusts how dark or light the instance appears. This won't affect the transparency of the symbol.

☆ **Tint** changes the overall color of the instance. Choose a color to apply to the symbol. A setting of 100% will override any color in the entire symbol with the new color. Any percentage less than that will mix the new color with the symbol's original colors.

☆ Use **Alpha** to make a symbol instance transparent. Set it to anything less than 100 and it will be semi-transparent. Set it to 0 and the symbol instance becomes invisible. You can make a symbol fade in or out by applying an Alpha value of 0 to the first or second keyframe.

☆ The **Advanced** settings allow you to combine Tint and Alpha effects.

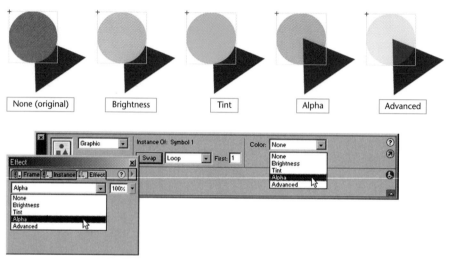

Figure 3.8 Different effects applied to an orange circle symbol instance. Use the Effect panel (the Properties Inspector for Flash MX) to modify a selected instance.

Creating a Fade-in with a Motion Tween

Use the Alpha effect to make an object on the Stage fade in or fade out.

☆ First, add a new layer to the Timeline.

☆ On that layer, add a keyframe and place a symbol instance (or convert an existing image to a symbol). Any behavior will do (graphic, movie clip, or button).

☆ Add a second keyframe several frames past the first keyframe. Flash will automatically duplicate the symbol instance from the first keyframe.

☆ Select the symbol instance in the first keyframe for a fade *in*, or select the instance in the second keyframe for a fade *out*. With the symbol instance selected, go to the Effects panel and change the Alpha value to 0%.

☆ When you're done, play the movie to see the fade.

Frame Panel Options for Motion Tween

When you select *Motion Tween* from the Frame panel, a few options appear.

☆ Normally, leave **Scale** checked for smooth tweening. If you uncheck this option, tweening will not apply to size changes. The tweened object would not change size gradually, but suddenly at the second keyframe.

☆ **Easing** changes the pace of the animation so that it accelerates or decelerates as it plays. By default, objects tween at a constant rate. This option can give motion a less uniform, more natural appearance. A bouncing ball can slow down as it reaches its apex. It may seem backwards, but a positive number for this option decelerates the transition and a negative number accelerates it.

☆ The **Rotate** option will send the tweened symbol spinning in either direction.

☆TIP   **Motion Tween with Text and Groups**

In place of a symbol, you can apply a motion tween to a block of text or to grouped objects. However, if you convert them to symbols, you would also benefit from other symbol features such as ease of editing.

◎◎ Creating a Shape Tween

While a motion tween animates symbol instances, a **shape tween** animates non-symbol, ungrouped objects. It **morphs** the shape from the first keyframe into the shape in the second keyframe, like turning a frown into a smile.

Shape tweens work with freestanding vector objects, not symbols or bitmap images. If you want to apply a shape tween to a symbol, you will have to select an instance of that symbol and choose Modify→Break Apart. This will convert a symbol into a simple Flash object. You also must ungroup any grouped objects (Modify→Ungroup).

Create a shape tween as you would a motion tween, except place a simple vector object in each keyframe. There can be any number of standard frames between the keyframes. Select the first keyframe and apply *Shape Tweening* from the Frame panel (the Properties Inspector in Flash MX). Look at the Timeline. Like a motion tween, the Timeline indicates a shape tween with an arrow (see Figure 3.6), except the shading is green.

To create the shape tween in Figure 3.9:

☆ Separate the object you want to shape tween and be sure to ungroup it and break it apart (A).

☆ Insert a keyframe for the end of tween (B).

☆ Manually reshape the art in the second keyframe (C).

☆ Assign a shape tween (D).

☆ Place shape hints, if needed (E).

☆ Add a second tween to bring the wings back to the start position, completing a loop (F).

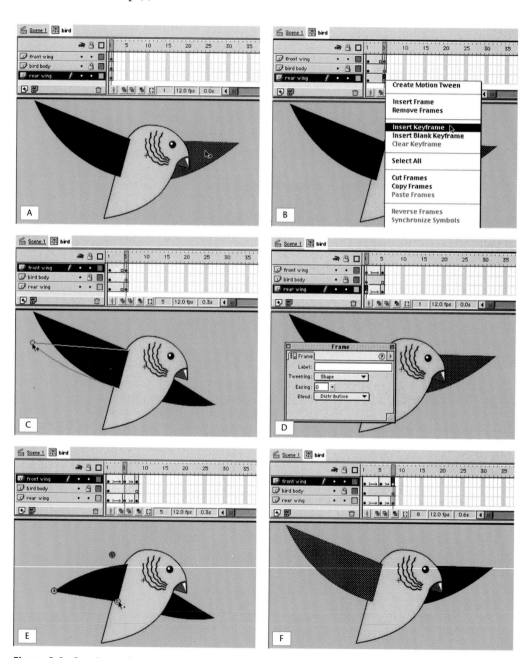

Figure 3.9 Creating a shape tween.

Shape Hints

Flash uses its own logic for tweening shapes. Sometimes, it may work just the way you want. Other times, you can give it some hints to do a better job. A shape hint instructs Flash that the point on the object at hint *a* in the first keyframe should match the point at hint *a* on the second keyframe. This helps to control a shape tween.

To add a shape hint, select the first keyframe of the shape tween. Then, choose the Modify→Transform→Add Shape Hint command (in Flash MX: Modify→Shape→Add Shape Hint). Repeat this command if you want to use more than one shape hint.

Each shape hint appears as a dot on the Stage, labeled by a letter of the alphabet. Move each dot to a key point on the shape you are tweening. When you go to the second keyframe, you should see the same number of shape hint dots, labeled with the same letters of the alphabet. Align each hint to a point on the shape corresponding to a point in the other keyframe.

Shape hints will only work aligned to a point on a path. A red dot indicates a hint that is not properly aligned. With either keyframe active, position the dots on the Stage until they are no longer red. The Stage should have yellow dots for the first keyframe and green dots for the second keyframe.

☆ **TIP**   **Disappearing Shape Hints**

The hints may seem to disappear at times, but they will still be doing their job. To reveal shape hints, choose View→Show Shape Hints.

Experiment with the location of each shape hint and move the frame indicator back and forth to see check the tween. Depending on where you place each hint, the tween will become smoother or more chaotic. To remove a shape hint, right-click (Ctrl-click for Macintosh) on the unwanted hint from the first keyframe of the tween and choose the Remove Hint command from the pop-up menu.

◎◎ Viewing Multiple Frames with Onion Skin

Normally, Flash displays one frame at a time in the Stage window. When you are creating animation or aligning objects for any reason, you may need to see how the Stage for the current frame relates to adjacent frames. You could check the position between frames by moving the frame indicator back and forth, but that's a fairly crude technique. Flash's **onion skin** feature allows you to view the contents of multiple frames simultaneously on the Stage.

Aligning Between Frames

Like keyframes and tweening, onion skinning has its roots in classic animation. An animator would draw successive frames on sheets of onion skin or vellum paper. These papers are translucent so that the frames on sheets underneath show through. Flash's onion skin feature mimics this. This can help you align objects in one keyframe to those in another keyframe, to create a smoother transition.

At the bottom of the Timeline, there are a few buttons (see Figure 3.10). Click on the first button, **Onion Skin**, and you will see semi-transparent or ghosted views from neighboring frames. Click on the second button, **Onion Skin Outlines**, and you will see the other frames as outlines rather than ghosts. The active frame (where the frame indicator is positioned) is not ghosted. If it is a keyframe, you can edit it.

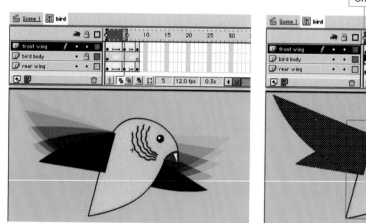
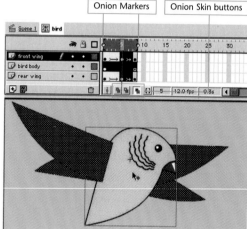

Figure 3.10 Onion skin view (left) and Edit Multiple Frames (right).

Changing the Range

Are enough frames or keyframes visible at once? You may have noticed the sliders and shading that appear with the frame indicator when you turn on Onion Skinning. These are the **Onion Markers**. They represent the range of frames that are visible at once. Click and drag the sliders to narrow or widen the visible range of frames.

Edit Multiple Frames

Normally in Flash you can view or edit only one keyframe at a time. Not only can you view more than one frame on the Stage with onion skinning, but also you can edit more than one keyframe. Depress the third button, **Edit Multiple Frames**, and you will be able to work with the objects from all visible keyframes.

If you want to change the composition of the entire Flash movie, depress the Edit Multiple Frames button. Also, open the Onion Markers all the way to the left and the right, and make sure all the layers are visible and unlocked. Choose Edit→Select All to select everything in sight. You can then drag the selection to move it all at once.

◎◎ Controlling Motion with Guide Layers

A guide layer is like a standard layer, except it doesn't appear in the final SWF file that you publish. Place or draw objects on a guide layer and use them as a reference for other layers. You could type comments to a guide layer to help you remember how you built the Flash movie. A guide layer can also be combined with another layer to change the path of a motion tween.

To convert any layer to a guide layer, double-click on the icon to the left of a layer name on the Timeline. This will open its Layer Properties window. Change the layer *Type*, to *Guide* and click the OK button (see Figure 3.11).

☆**TIP**   **Hiding Content**

Guide layers may be visible while you work, but they are not visible in the SWF file movie that you publish. Conversely, non-guide layers are visible no matter what. Even if you hide a standard layer and save the file, it still will be visible in the SWF file you publish. If you want to hide a layer from the published movie, convert it to a guide layer.

Setting up a Motion Guide

By default, a motion tween will move a symbol from point A to point B along a straight path. It doesn't have to move straight if you add a motion guide.

On the Timeline select a layer with a motion tween and choose Insert→Motion Guide (or click the Add Guide Layer button, labeled in Figure 3.11). This will append a motion guide layer to the selected layer. You don't need to add any keyframes to the guide layer. Just draw a line with the Pencil or Pen tool. This line is the motion guide, the path for the animation.

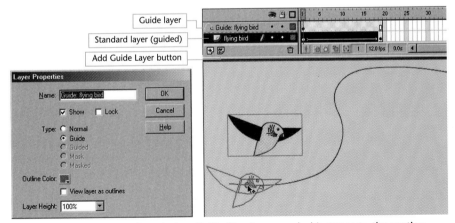

Figure 3.11 Layer Properties window (left). Aligning a symbol instance to the motion guide (right).

The center point of the symbol must align with the motion guide in each keyframe. Drag the symbol instance in the first keyframe of the motion tween until its crosshairs align with the guide. A larger circle will appear at the crosshairs when it is aligned (see Figure 3.11). Go to the second keyframe and align that instance of the symbol to a different location on the same path. Play your movie and the animation should follow the path.

If the symbol doesn't follow the path, it may not be aligned to the path. Repeat the alignment process in the previous paragraph. You can check the Snap box on the Frame panel to help you. Also, make sure it is *not* a closed path.

Tweaking the Path

You can change the orientation of the symbol instance as it follows the guide path. With the symbol instance in the first keyframe selected, check *Orient to Path* on the Frame panel. With this option, the symbol instance will rotate left and right in the direction of the path as it moves.

You can also move the crosshairs (or center point) which determines how the symbol instance is centered along the path. With the symbol instance selected, choose Modify→Transform→Edit Center and drag its crosshairs to a new location. Then realign the center point to the motion guide path.

> ☆ **FLASH MX   Using the Free Transform Tool to Reposition the Center Point**
>
> In Flash MX, select a symbol instance with the Free Transform tool to reposition its center point.

Once you have created a motion guide and are satisfied with it, you can hide it like any other layer. This will reduce clutter when you're trying to edit other parts of the movie, but it will still guide the motion.

Using Layer Properties to Create a Motion Guide

If you want to convert an existing layer into a motion guide layer, double-click its icon on the Timeline. This will open the Layer Properties window where you can choose *Guide* as its type. Once it is converted to a guide layer, drag a normal layer right on top of the guide layer and it will become linked to the guide layer. If you want to unlink a layer from a guide layer, just drag it above the guide layer (or change its Type to *Normal* from the Layer Properties window).

◎◎ Applying Mask Layers

A mask layer can hide and reveal selected areas of other layers. As you add multiple layers to the Flash movie, you can use a mask layer to control how they are combined. Confine a bitmap image or any object to a specific shape or area.

Create a Mask

A mask layer can be grouped with another layer, or with multiple layers. To create a mask layer, add a new layer just above the layer you want to mask. Then draw a solid shape of the area you want to reveal (it doesn't matter what color). It can even be a symbol instance. The mask will reveal the area of the shape and hide everything else.

After setting it up, right-click ([Ctrl]-click for Macintosh) on the mask layer and choose *Mask* from the pop-up menu. The mask layer is now masking the layer just below it.

Working with Masks

If you want to change something on a mask layer or the layer it masks at a later time, first unlock it. When you are finished, right-click ([Ctrl]-click for Macintosh) on the mask layer and choose *Show Masking*, to see how the mask looks (see Figure 3.12).

You can mask more than one layer with a single mask. Just drag any other layer name directly below the mask layer name. Any unmasked layers below those layers will show through, outside of the mask shape.

Figure 3.12 The blue circle is on the mask layer (left) and the abstract pattern is on the layer it is masking. The same Stage with Show Masking enabled (right).

Animating a Mask

☆ To give a spotlight effect, apply a motion tween to the mask. As it moves, it will reveal different parts of what it masks.

☆ To give a porthole effect, apply a motion tween to the layer that is masked. The mask in the foreground stays still, while the masked artwork moves inside it.

☆ If you want to move the mask and a masked object together, you'll have to tween each layer separately.

◎◎ Managing Assets in the Library

Every Flash movie has its own library. The library is a repository for all of the **assets** of a movie: symbols, imported bitmap images, sounds. Choose Window→Library to open it. When you are building a movie, you place instances of these library assets on the Stage. Each instance refers to a corresponding asset in the library.

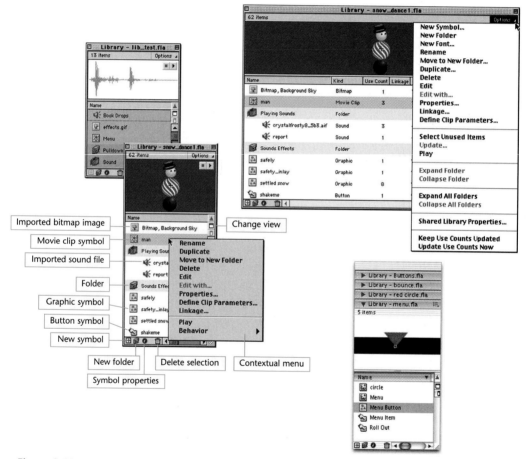

Figure 3.13 A collapsed view (left) and an expanded view (right) of the library. At the bottom right is the Flash MX library in the Macintosh OS X version of Flash.

☆ FLASH MX   Docking Libraries

In Flash MX, multiple libraries can be docked together like other panels (see Figure 3.13). They can even be docked with other panels.

Symbols

Every symbol instance on the Stage of a Flash movie refers to an original symbol in the library. The full inventory of symbols for a Flash movie is listed in the library panel. From this list, double-click on a symbol icon to edit that symbol. Drag the symbol name or its preview from the library onto the Stage to create a new instance of it.

In the library, you can edit the properties of a symbol such as its behavior (graphic, button, movie clip) or change its name. You can duplicate an existing symbol or create a new one from scratch. Select a symbol from the library's list and change its properties from the Options pop-up menu at the top right of the library panel. Right-click ([Ctrl]-click for Macintosh) on a symbol name to reveal a contextual menu with several choices. (See Figure 3.13.)

Other Assets

The library also organizes imported bitmap images and sounds. It even accepts imported movie clips. All of these become assets in a movie's library. Flash handles these assets a lot like symbols. You can place instances of these assets throughout the movie from the library, or even tween them. Each instance refers to the original image or sound in the library.

☆ **FLASH MX**   **Import to Library**

In Flash MX, you can import an image file directly to the library. Use the command File→Import to Library if you aren't ready to place it on the Stage.

Double-click on the icon of any asset in the library to change its properties. Bitmap properties allow you to decide how you want each image compressed when the Flash movie is exported and published as a SWF file. Sound files in the library can also have their own compression settings. See Chapter Six for more about compression settings.

Organizing the Library

If you're only using a handful of symbols or other assets, you don't need to worry too much about library management. If you build a Flash movie that's more complex, the library can easily grow to dozens of items.

As your library increases in size, the names of the symbols become more important. You want to use short, but descriptive names. By default, Flash sorts the library alphabetically. If you're building a cartoon cat from several symbols, you may want to name them all in the same manner so that they are sorted together (e.g., cat claw, cat paw, cat tail).

You can organize symbols with folders. In the cat example, you can add a folder named "cat" and add symbols, sounds, and bitmap images to it.

☆ Choose *New Folder* from the Options menu to add an untitled folder icon to the library.

☆ Double-click the folder icon to open or close it.

☆ Double-click its name to rename it.

☆ Drag a symbol or asset over the folder to add it to the folder.

☆ Drag items outside the folder to remove them from the folder.

☆**TIP   Symbolic Housecleaning**

Flash will not export unused symbols to the SWF files you publish, but the clutter in the library makes managing symbols more difficult and adds to the size of the work file. Flash makes it easy to remove this debris with the *Select Unused Items* command from the Options pull-down menu. After it has selected the items, choose *Delete* from the same menu. In some cases, you may have to do this more than once if any symbols are nested.

Sharing Libraries

Libraries are your repositories for symbols, images, and sounds. Not only can you reuse these attributes in a single movie, but you can share them between different movies.

Dragging Between Libraries

When more than one Flash file is open at once, you can copy symbols and other assets between their libraries. Open two or more libraries and drag assets between them to copy them. You can also copy an asset from the Stage of one movie and paste it to a second movie. The asset will be automatically added to the library of the second movie.

Open as Library

If you need a file only for its library, you can open it by choosing File→Open as Library. This will open only the library panel for a movie, not its Stage or Timeline.

Adding a Permanent Library to the Flash Program

Create a library of frequently used symbols that are accessible any time you use Flash. Save a Flash file with the library and place it in the Libraries folder inside the Flash program folder on your computer. The libraries of any files placed there will be available from the Window→Common Libraries submenu.

☆**TIP   Which Library Is Active?**

With several libraries open at once, it can be a little confusing to tell which library belongs to which movie. The library for the active movie has a white background. All other libraries are shaded gray (see Figure 3.13, upper left). Each library is labeled by its corresponding filename to identify it.

Publishing Shared Libraries

If you are creating a site with several Flash movies, they may share some of the same assets. You can set up a library of symbols, sounds, and bitmap images that other Flash movies can link to. This is a more advanced feature of Flash. If you would like to learn how to use it, see the Online References at the end of this chapter.

◎◎ Adding Scenes to the Movie

By default, every Flash movie has one scene. Flash allows you to add multiple scenes as an organizational tool. You can break your movie into logical blocks with different settings like scenes in a play. They play in succession from the first scene on, or they can be called out of order by Actions. You can add a scene as an introductory page or a loading sequence (see Chapter Six).

The main Timeline of any movie shows one scene at a time. From the scene panel, you can move, add, remove, rename, and change the order of scenes. You may also use it to navigate between scenes.

☆ WARNING   Avoid Multiple Scenes

Multiple scenes are not a requirement for making a successful Flash movie. In fact, it's best to avoid them. You could use this feature to separate an introduction from the rest of the movie, but multiple scenes can cause problems with the main content of your Flash movie. Many actions have trouble with multiple scenes. It's better to use the one default scene for the entire movie, or divide a larger project into multiple movies and link them with the *Load Movie* or *Get URL* actions (covered in Chapter Four).

Adding Scenes to the Movie

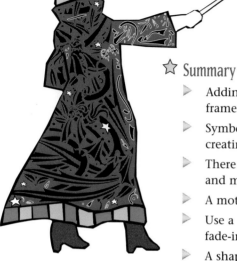

☆ Summary

- ▷ Adding keyframes to the Timeline allows you to create frame-by-frame animation.

- ▷ Symbols and their instances are the building blocks for creating more efficient animation.

- ▷ There are three types of symbol behavior: graphic, button, and movie clip.

- ▷ A motion tween automates animation.

- ▷ Use a motion tween for other visual effects such as a fade-in.

- ▷ A shape tween automates the transition between two non-symbol objects.

- ▷ The onion skin feature helps you to view or edit more than one frame at a time on the Stage.

- ▷ Use guide layers to manipulate the path of an animation.

- ▷ Masking layers allows certain parts of a layer to be hidden and other parts to be revealed.

- ▷ Manage symbols and other assets from the Library.

- ▷ Avoid adding multiple scenes to a Flash movie.

☆ Online References

Optimizing Flash Animations
`http://www.webmonkey.com/01/04/index0a.html`

Creating Flash Animations in Freehand
`http://www.macromedia.com/support/freehand/programs/creating_animations`

Creating a Walk Cycle in Flash
`http://www.webmonkey.com/02/05/index4a.html`

A Scientific Explanation of Motion Tween Animation
`http://www.cs.brown.edu/stc/outrea/greenhouse/nursery/interpolation/formal.html`

Shape Hint Tutorial
`http://www.orionnetlinks.com/Flash/shape03.asp`

Web Animation Guide
`http://webguide.awn.com`

Animation Bibliography
`http://www.tcp.com/~bigboote/biblio.html`

Animation Definitions
http://www.cs.brown.edu/stc/summer/94Animation/
94Animation_1.html

Shockwave Animation and Entertainment Web site.
http://www.shockwave.com

Using Shared Libraries
http://www.macromedia.com/support/flash/ts/documents/
shared_libraries.htm

☆ Review Questions

1. Where do changes occur on the Timeline?
2. What is the least efficient animation technique that uses many keyframes?
3. What is the most efficient animation technique that uses only two keyframes?
4. What is a symbol?
5. What do you place on the Stage: a symbol or a symbol instance? Which is placed in the library?
6. Which type of symbol behavior would you use to create a ball that spins independent of the main movie?
7. What effect do you apply to a symbol to change its color?
8. How do you make one shape transform gradually into another shape?
9. How do you reposition everything on the Stage of a Flash movie at once?
10. What type of layers are visible only while you work?

☆ Hands-On Exercises

1. Create a frame-by-frame animation of 20 frames. Set the movie's frame rate to 4 frames per second. Change the movie's background color to any color but white.
2. Create a two-layer symbol from scratch. Add a new layer to the main Timeline of the movie and place 10 or more instances of that symbol on the Stage (as in Figure 6.1). Then, edit that symbol to change all 10 instances at once.
3. Add a second layer to the movie and create a motion tween animation. Then add a guide layer to control the direction of the motion. Extend the animation to create a fade-out of the symbol.
4. Add a third layer and create a shape tween. Add shape hints to control the tween.
5. Import a bitmap image into the same Flash movie. Place it on top of all the other layers. Add a mask layer to reveal only part of that layer.

CHAPTER FOUR

BASIC ACTIONS

I f you've completed the previous chapters, you should know your way around Flash pretty well by now. You have learned how to draw something in Flash and make it dance. If you threw this book away right now, you'd be able to make some pretty cool animations. But why stop there? This chapter adds interactivity through basic actions. After all, don't you want to make something for your audience to click on?

◎◎ Chapter Objectives

☆ Introduce interactivity
☆ Add and test a simple frame action
☆ Create a button symbol and apply a play action
☆ Apply other essential actions
☆ Learn to use the *Tell Target* action to control movie clips
☆ Build a pull-down menu

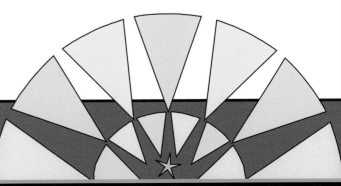

◎◎ Interactivity in Flash

The techniques you have learned up to this point have been concentrated on creating something visual. Chapter Two focused on drawing and manipulating graphics. Chapter Three was mostly about animation. You can do a lot of great stuff with just those skills, and some of it is very entertaining. But that's a more passive experience: The movie plays to the audience like a film in a projector.

Flash can also be an active experience. By applying actions, a designer can construct a Flash movie that does something more than just playing straight through from the first frame to the last. The Flash movie can create a dialog with its users wherever they click, type, and otherwise interact with it. This allows the users some control of what happens when the Flash movie plays, giving them individualized experiences.

Depending on how it is designed, an interactive experience allows the audience to start and stop or play a movie out of sequence. You can create more complex animations with some actions, and start and stop sounds. The more advanced examples allow users to move things around the screen, create new objects, or play games.

What Is ActionScript?

To be technical, all actions in Flash are a form of ActionScript, which is a programming language specific to Flash. In Chapter Seven you'll learn how to write actions or scripts by hand using ActionScript. It's those handwritten scripts that are usually referred to as ActionScript.

This chapter focuses on a few basic actions that will allow you to do things such as make the movie jump to a specific frame or stop altogether. Later on in this chapter, you'll learn how to do other things such as loading one movie within another and stopping and starting the animation in a movie clip. You won't have to know a bit of ActionScript to apply the actions covered in this chapter.

Two Ways to Trigger an Action

In Flash, no action can occur unless something triggers it, such as pressing a button. An **event** triggers every action. The event doesn't determine what the action does, but regulates when it occurs.

Essentially, there are two types of events in Flash: movie events and user events. A movie event is triggered automatically by the movie, such as when it reaches a particular frame. A user event, such as a mouse click, is often assigned to a button.

To assign an action in Flash, you'll need to first create a keyframe on the Timeline or place a symbol instance on the Stage. In this chapter, you'll be selecting either a keyframe for a movie event or a button for a user event and appending actions to it.

◎◎ The Actions Panel

Any time you write an action in Flash—simple or complex—you'll use the Actions panel. In the Actions panel, you view existing actions as well as create new ones. It's where you spend most of your time while creating actions in Flash. If the Actions panel is not visible, choose Window→Actions to open it.

☆ SHORTCUT **Opening the Actions Panel**

Double-click on a keyframe to open the Actions panel in Flash 5. Or press Ctrl-Alt-A (⌘-Option-A for Macintosh). In Flash MX, use the F9 key to open the Actions panel.

As with other panels, the options menu for the Actions panel is accessed from the top right corner of the panel. One of the options lets you choose between *Normal* mode and *Expert* mode. (The other options are for checking your code and are more relevant for when you are working in Expert mode.)

In the Normal mode, you don't need to know how to write ActionScript code. This mode offers menus with simple choices and writes the ActionScript for you in the text pane. It's a safer way to work and makes it harder to make mistakes. You choose a basic action from one menu and change its **parameters** from other menus below. For this chapter, we'll use Normal mode. In Chapter Seven, you'll be using the Expert mode to type directly in the text pane.

Click on the add (or plus) button to add an action or statement. Any action you choose from this menu will be added to the main text pane of the Actions panel. To remove an action, select it in the text pane and then click the minus button.

☆ SHORTCUT **Hiding the Actions Pane**

Flash gives you a divided window with all the selectable actions listed in the left pane. All of these options are also available under the add (plus sign) menu, so this pane is not essential. You can close it by clicking on the divider between the two panes (see Figure 4.1). To reveal it later, click on the divider again.

Most actions require parameters. Parameters adapt an action to a specific situation, such as telling the movie which frame in the Timeline to jump to. In the parameters pane of the panel (see Figure 4.1), you set attributes that are specific to each action. This is only available in the Normal mode.

◎◎ Frame Actions

A frame action is triggered by the movie itself. It doesn't matter what the user does. If an action has been assigned to a keyframe in frame 20 of the movie, it will execute invariably whenever the movie plays frame 20.

Often, frame actions are coupled with object actions. Let's say you want your movie to stop right at the beginning, at the very first frame, where it prompts the user to click a button. Add a *Stop* action to the first keyframe and the movie will not play past it. On the same frame, you would add a button action to get the movie moving. Your users could either ignore the button or click it. They control what happens.

Frame Actions

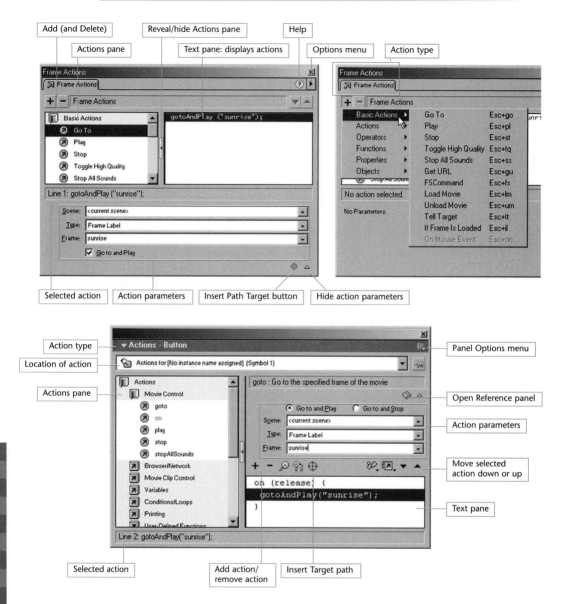

Figure 4.1 The Actions panel with a simple action (top left), and revealing the Basic Actions menu (top right). Below is the Flash MX Actions panel.

This is a very simple interaction, but it's a standard one that you might use again and again. Some more complex interactions build on the same structure: The frame action does one thing automatically, and then the user decides to do another.

Assigning a Frame Action: Stop

To try this out, open a movie where you have created an animation. An exercise from Chapter Three will do. To assign a *Stop* action, select the first keyframe (any layer will do). With that keyframe selected, choose Basic Actions→Stop from the add (plus) menu in the Actions panel. In the text pane of the Actions panel you should now see:

```
stop();
```

That's the ActionScript that the Flash program wrote for you. Congratulations—if you did this, you have created an action in Flash. The *Stop* action is the simplest one in Flash and it's used a lot.

☆ **WARNING Stop the Loop**

By default, a Flash movie will repeat endlessly. This often isn't what you want. Add a keyframe with a *Stop* action to the last frame of a movie to prevent it from looping (replaying) automatically.

◎◎ Checking Your Actions

Since you've created your first *Stop* action, you probably want to see what it does. You should check your work each time you assign an action. The Control menu offers you several preview options. For checking actions, Control→Enable Simple Frame Actions and Control→Enable Simple Buttons allow you to preview some actions right on the Stage as you work.

However, the Stage preview is limited. Some actions and symbols won't work here or they won't work the same way as your audience will see it. Choose Control→Test Movie to enter the preview mode of Flash. Use Ctrl-Enter (⌘-Enter) for Macintosh) on your keyboard as a shortcut. Chapter Six goes into more depth about the preview feature.

If you added the *Stop* action described in the previous section, see what happens (or doesn't) when you preview it. The animation should not play.

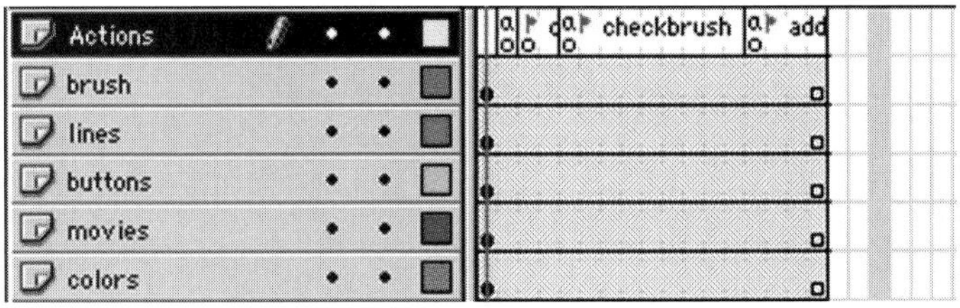

Figure 4.2 Frame actions are indicated in the Timeline by the small letter "a." Labels are indicated by red flags and the label itself, as it fits.

> ☆ **TIP**   Actions Layer
>
> Frame actions are assigned independent of anything on the Stage. You assign them to the Timeline because that's where the frames are. In most cases, it doesn't matter which layer in the Timeline you use. As your movies grow in complexity, however, you may have trouble finding the actions if you apply them to assorted layers.
>
> Add a separate layer to the movie and reserve it just for frame actions. It's no different than any other layer except that you decide to only place actions in it, no symbol instances or other art. You can also add frame labels (covered later in this chapter) to this same layer. This makes it clear where all your frame actions are (see Figure 4.2).

◎◎ Button Actions

While frame actions are initiated by the movie itself, button actions are triggered by someone interacting with the movie. When you create a button action, you are giving your audience a choice. The audience always has the choice to ignore the button, but who can resist clicking? You could create a series of buttons that offer several options as well, like the sections of a Web site.

Any image can be a button in Flash. If you want to be sure that most people will click on your button, you will want to make it apparent that your button is click-able (see Figure 4.3). One example is to create a 3-dimensional illusion such as shadowing; another is to add a small icon such as the Options menu triangles on the Flash 5 panels.

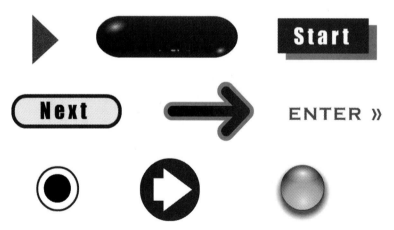

Figure 4.3 Examples of button icons.

Creating a Button Symbol

The button symbol is unique. A graphic symbol or movie clip symbol has a Timeline identical to the main Timeline of the entire Flash movie. A button symbol has a specific four-frame Timeline. The four frames help you create a button that responds visually to a mouse.

Each of the four frames has a built-in action that you cannot change. The frames designate how the button appears when the mouse is *over* the button or clicks *down* on it.

Button Frame	Purpose of Frame
Up	What the button looks like when there is no interaction, when the mouse is not over it.
Over	What the button looks like when the mouse hovers over the button, but does not click on it.
Down	What the button looks like when the mouse clicks down on the button.
Hit	The area of the button that will respond to the mouse. The Over and Down states and any actions assigned to the button will occur only when the mouse is in the area you define in this frame. This is like an image map in HTML.

To create a new button, start with the Insert→New Symbol command. Select *Button* behavior for the new symbol. That will bring you to a blank Stage and the button Timeline with exactly four frames.

It's usually best to start with the *Up* frame and insert the other keyframes after that one is done. That will allow you to modify what was in the *Up* frame rather than starting from scratch for each frame. While you are confined to the four keyframes for a button symbol, you may add as many layers as you wish. If you want to add text, add another layer. (See Figure 4.4.)

Buttons with Fewer than Four Keyframes

Although it's recommended that you create separate art for each of a button's four frames, it's not required. You can create just the *Up* keyframe, and a button symbol can still receive actions. It just won't respond visually when the mouse rolls over or clicks on it. Add an *Over* keyframe and the button will respond to the mouse. In this case, the *Down* and *Hit* frames will automatically inherit what's in the *Over* frame.

To make an invisible button, add just a *Hit* keyframe. Keep the *Up* and other frames empty. When you place this button on the Stage within Flash, it will appear as a transparent blue to help you position it. However, it will be completely invisible in the published SWF file. Add an invisible button that covers the entire Stage and a user can click anywhere to trigger an action.

Nesting Other Symbols in Buttons

Remember, symbol nesting in Chapter Three? You can place an instance of the same graphic symbol for each of the four button states. Then modify each instance from the Effects panel (Properties Inspector from Flash MX). Or place an animated movie clip symbol in the *Over* frame and your button will come alive as the mouse rolls over it.

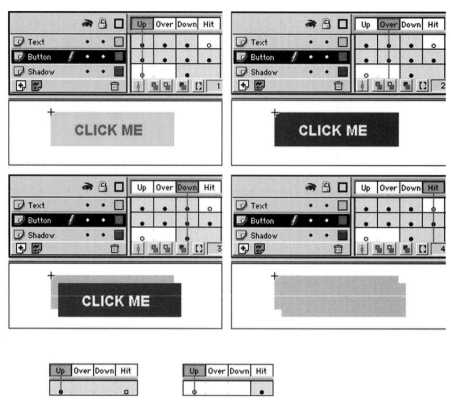

Figure 4.4 The four frames of a button symbol (top). Below are the Timelines for a one-frame button and an invisible button.

Preview a Button

To preview a button symbol, you must place an instance on the Stage in the main Timeline of the movie. Go to the Library panel, select the button, and drag it onto the Stage to create an instance. If it's a simple button with no nested movie clip symbols, you can choose Control→Enable Simple Buttons. Then roll your mouse over it and click to your heart's delight. Of course, Control→Test Movie is the most accurate way to preview it.

Adding a Button Action: Play

An earlier section in this chapter described how to add a frame action to stop an animation at the first frame. Leave the movie like that and it would just sit there all day. Add a *Play* action to the button and the person viewing the movie (the user) can make the animation play.

First, drag an instance of a button symbol onto the Stage of the same file. It looks like a button and responds to the mouse, but it doesn't do anything else. You need to wire it up with an action.

You add an action to a button just like you would to a keyframe, except select a button. With the button selected, go to the Actions panel. (If you had chosen *Enable Simple Buttons* earlier, you'll have to choose it again to disable it.) Choose Basic Actions→Play (Actions→Movie Control→play for Flash MX) from the Add Action (plus sign) menu.

Now your button has a *Play* action. When you test the movie, it should be stopped at first. Click the button and it should play.

Assigning a Mouse Event

When you add an action to a button, you must specify how it will be triggered. This is the *event*. In Normal mode, Flash automatically inserts `on (release)` for any actions assigned to a button to ensure that it works properly. This part of the action, called an **event handler**, defines how the button will trigger the play action.

After adding the Play action to a button, you should see this in the text pane:

```
on (release) {
    play ();
}
```

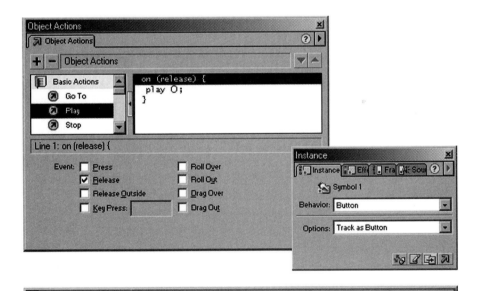

Figure 4.5 Assigning a mouse event from the parameters pane. Setting button behavior from the Instance panel in Flash 5 or the Properties Inspector in Flash MX.

In Normal mode, select a line of the code in the text pane and different menus, checkboxes, or input boxes will appear in the Actions panel. These represent parameters or settings for the selected line of script.

The `play()` action is very simple and has no parameters. Select `on (release)` and you will see several options, labeled *Events*. Since there are several ways someone could interact with a button, Flash allows several different choices here. You can select as many events or as few as you want, but you must select at least one.

Checked by default, *Release* is the event just after a mouse click down, when the button is released. If that's the event you need, then your work is done. If you want the action to occur when the mouse drags over the button, check *Drag Over*.

This table explains all of the different mouse events that Flash recognizes. Rather than memorizing this table, try them out and test the movie.

Mouse Event	Description of Event
Press	While the mouse is over the symbol instance, the mouse button is clicked down.
Release	After a Press, when the mouse is released over the symbol.
Release Outside	After a Press, when the mouse is released outside the symbol.
Key Press	A specific key on the keyboard is pressed. The window with the button symbol must have been clicked on already.
Roll Over	With no key depressed, the mouse moves over the symbol.
Roll Out	With no key depressed, the mouse moves outside the symbol.
Drag Over	Click-down outside symbol and drag into it.
Drag Out	Click-down inside symbol and drag outside it.

Setting Button Behavior

Flash requires that your symbol have button behavior in order to accept actions. However, your symbol doesn't have to be a button symbol. Confused?

Sometimes you may want a button to be obvious and react to the mouse, and other times you may want less obvious buttons. Button behavior is assigned in two places: to the original symbol itself and to every instance of the symbol that you place on the Stage. Change a graphic symbol to a button symbol in the library to give it the four button frames: Up, Over, Down, Hit. If a graphic symbol looks fine as is and you just want to assign actions, assign button behavior to a single instance.

Change an original symbol's overall behavior via its properties settings under the library's Options menu. Change a single instance from the Behavior menu on the Instance panel. (See Figure 3.3.) It doesn't matter what the original symbol is set to, but an instance must be set to *Button* behavior to accept actions.

☆ **FLASH MX**   No Instance or Frame Panels

In Flash MX, the Properties Inspector replaces the Instance and Frame panels. When you select a symbol instance, the instance options will be available in the Properties Inspector panel. When you select a frame in the Timeline, the frame options become available there.

Movie Clip Events

Since version 5, Flash has supported movie clip events as well. You can assign an event based on the behavior of the movie clip or different kinds of user interaction. This has opened the door to accurately tracking the mouse amongst other things. Consult the Flash manual for a list of clip events.

☆ **FLASH MX**   New Events for Flash MX

Flash MX adds several objects that allow you to assign behavior just like a button to a movie clip. With *onRollover, onRelease,* and others you could create a button out of a movie clip. This version also adds new events to sounds and the mouse. See a Flash MX reference for more about these events.

◎◎ Applying a Few More Basic Actions

You should now be familiar with the *Play* and *Stop* actions, the most basic actions in Flash. Flash has several other basic actions built into it. You don't need to touch ActionScript to use these either, but they can create some impressive interactivity.

Go To

With no actions, a Flash movie will play straight through from the first frame to the last. The *Stop* action, discussed in the previous section, interrupts this. The *Go To* action allows a movie to play frames out of order, in a nonlinear fashion. It tells the movie to jump to a specific frame. Assign separate *Go To* actions to more than one button, and you allow your user to decide where the movie goes.

If you haven't labeled a keyframe yet, you need to do so from the Frame panel. Select the target keyframe for this action on the Timeline and type something into the Label field of the Frame panel (Properties Inspector for Flash MX). A short and descriptive name works best; keep it to just one word if possible. Use a different name to label each keyframe or you will get unexpected results from your actions.

Once assigned to a button or frame, there are a few parameters for this action. These are the ones you should change:

☆ Select the *Go to and Play* option so that the movie will continue playing from the targeted frame.

☆ Under the Type field on the Actions panel, choose *Frame Label*.

Once you choose that option, all the labeled keyframes on the movie's main Timeline become available in the Frame field. Choose a label to complete this action.

You could use the Frame Number parameter for the *Go To* action and get the same result, but if you later added frames or shifted them in the Timeline, you'd have to change the frame number in the action. Flash will go to the specified frame number no matter what keyframe is there. If you are referring to a label, you can count on that label staying with the same keyframe, even if you move it.

Get URL

While the *Go To* action navigates within a Flash movie, the *Get URL* action can link to anywhere on the Web. You could create an entire set of buttons in Flash to use as navigation for a traditional HTML Web site. In Flash, the *Get URL* action allows you to apply a Web link to any button.

After you add a *Get URL* link to a button, go to the parameters area of the Actions panel:

 In the URL field, type the address of any Web page either on the same site or another site.

 The Window parameter is optional. This controls what window or frame will load the URL. If you know something about HTML, this is the same as the TARGET parameter in HTML links. Leave it alone to load the Web page in the same window or frame as the Flash movie. Enter *_blank* and a new window will pop open with the link. Or if you have created a framed Web page, you can load that link into a named frame.

JavaScript is a language for applying actions to standard HTML Web pages. See the *Web Wizard's Guide to JavaScript* to learn how to use it. You can enter a short script in the URL field in place of an HTML link. This will pop open a remote window:

```
javascript:window.open('http://www.mysite.com/menu.html',
'menu','width=200,height=100');
```

Load Movie

As your Flash project grows, you could build it out by combining separate movies. Create soundtrack and navigational components as their own movies and load them into the main movie with the *Load Movie* action. This also allows you to break up a large Flash project into bite-size pieces.

The main movie could have several different buttons that allow users to load their choice of movies or soundtracks. Only what they choose will be loaded. If you know how to use HTML frames, it's a lot like a Web page with links that load different content into a particular frame.

This action takes a little more planning than the previous ones. You first need to save multiple SWF movie files for one project. One is the main movie that plays first, loading the other movies into it. See Chapter Six to learn more about exporting SWF files.

Load Movie does not allow you to specify the position of the movies. They will be positioned based on their upper left-hand corners. The easiest way around this is to create two same-sized movies so that you can see the alignment better. In each movie, leave space for the elements of the other movie so that their elements align (see Figure 4.6).

To apply this action, add a *Load Movie* action to the main movie. Select Load Movie from the Basic Actions submenu on the Actions panel (Actions→ Browser/Network→loadMovie for Flash MX).

These are the parameters that you should pay attention to for this action:

☆ The URL parameter is the name of the file you are loading. Enter it here.

☆ Select *Level* for the Location parameter.

☆ Enter the number *1* next to Level.

Figure 4.6 Aligning movies. Movie A loads movie B, displaying like C.

You should see something like this in the text pane of the Actions panel:

```
loadMovieNum ("portfolio3.swf", 1);
```

It's essential that the URL field reflect where the movie will be when it is eventually published on the Web. Otherwise the action would fail. It's best to put both the original SWF file and the loaded one in the same location, because you can link to it with a simple URL such as *filename.swf*.

Every movie loaded into Flash occupies a numbered level, 0 or greater. When a movie first loads, it occupies Level 0 by default. If you enter *0* as the Level parameter, the loaded movie will replace the original one. A level with a greater number will appear in front of a level with a lesser number, much like layers. Other than that, the exact number is not important.

The *Unload Movie* action will remove any loaded movie. Direct this action to the numbered level where you have previously loaded a movie and it will be removed.

Look for an example of the *Load Movie* action and other actions in this chapter on the Web Wizard Web site: `http://www.aw.com/webwizard`.

☆ **FLASH MX**   **Loading Images and Sounds**

Flash MX allows you to also load JPEG images with *Load Movie*. Just specify the URL of a JPEG file. This allows you to update images outside of Flash without having to save a new SWF file each time. When the action is called, the image will load. MP3 sound files may also be loaded similarly in Flash MX using the *Load Sound* action.

◎◎ Controlling Movie Clips with Tell Target

The full power of Flash actions comes from combining different symbol instances, sounds, and actions. Chapter Seven explains how ActionScript can combine various sets of actions and symbols to create myriad possibilities. *Tell Target* doesn't require ActionScript wizardry, and it allows you to expand the realm of basic actions. Also, it lays the foundation for learning how to write ActionScript in Chapter Seven.

Tell Target does just what its name infers. It *tells* the *target* symbol instance or movie what to do. It provides the means to send an action from a button or keyframe to another object such as a movie clip instance or a loaded movie. A *Tell Target* action can make an animation or sound stop or start. This section will take you through the process of creating such an action.

Setting Up a Movie Clip as a Target

The movie clip symbol is an essential ingredient of *Tell Target* actions. A movie clip instance also allows you to name it and *Tell Target* requires a name to identify its target.

In this example, the movie clip is also essential because you are going to create a looping animation. Since a movie clip can animate even if the main movie is stopped, this will work even if the main Timeline is stopped.

First, create a movie clip animation in a new Flash file. If you need a refresher, see the section on animating symbols in Chapter Three. Place an instance of the movie clip animation on the main Stage of the movie.

Name the movie clip from the Instance panel (Properties Inspector for Flash MX). This name is the one that is used in the actions and is distinct from the symbol name that you see in the library. Like keyframe labels, you should keep the name short and descriptive. It is best to keep it to one word. You can connect multiple words with an underscore. Name this instance *animate_me*.

☆ **FLASH MX**   **Naming Buttons**

Flash MX allows you to name button instances. This allows them to be the target of actions too.

Adding the Tell Target Action

Once you have placed a named movie clip instance on the Stage, you can create a *Tell Target* action. A *Tell Target* can be assigned to a frame action or an object action. In this example, a *Tell Target* is assigned to a button.

Create the button symbol and place an instance of it on the Stage. The button can be on a different layer than the movie clip, but it must appear at the same time. Add a *Stop* action to the keyframe where they both appear. The main Timeline of the movie will be still, but the symbols can communicate.

With the button symbol selected, use an *On Mouse Event* from the Action panel to add a Release event. Then add a *Tell Target* action to that. You should see the following in the text pane:

```
on (release) {
    tellTarget ("") {
    }
}
```

Assigning the Target

The path is the crux of a *Tell Target* action. It is the only parameter. It links the action to the target, a movie clip in this case. While writing a *Tell Target* action, the Target field appears as the only parameter in the Actions panel. This is where you assign the path.

If the button action and target movie clip instance are both on the main Timeline, the target path is simply the name of the instance. This is the case for this example. If the target movie clip instance is named *animate_me*, type that in the Target field. A later section of this chapter explains in depth how to use paths.

Applying the Tell Target Action

Once you have assigned a path to the target, you can add an action to control the target movie clip. In this case, add a *Stop* action just below the *Tell Target* action (see Figure 4.7). When someone clicks on that button, it should tell the targeted movie clip animation to stop playing. Choose the Control→Test Movie command (or Ctrl-Enter for Windows, ⌘-Enter for Macintosh) to try it out.

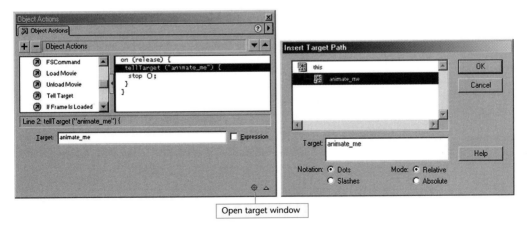

Figure 4.7 Setting the path for a Tell Target action.

In the text pane, it is essential to place the *Stop* action between the curly braces of (nested within) the *Tell Target* action. Both actions are also nested within the *On Mouse Event* action (see Figure 4.7). If they are not, you can reorder them by dragging the actions up and down in the text pane.

Duplicating a Symbol with Its Action

An animation with a Stop button is pretty much a dud once you've clicked the button. To make this better, add a Play button. There's no need to start from scratch. You can duplicate a button instance the same way you would any other object in Flash: With the Alt key on the keyboard depressed (Option key for Macintosh), drag the instance to create a new one. (Or, you copy and paste the button with the Edit menu.)

Select the duplicated button instance and go to the Actions panel. Since the button's actions were duplicated too, so you should see something familiar there, the action you created for the original button instance. This is going to be a *Play* button rather than a *Stop* button, so replace the *Stop* action with a *Play* action. Select `stop();` in the text area and click the Delete button (the minus sign). Next, select the `tellTarget()` line and add a *Play* action from the Basic Actions menu (the *Actions* menu in Flash MX). Selecting the `tellTarget()` action first ensures that the *Play* action will be nested within it.

```
on(release) {
    tellTarget("animate_me") {
    play();
    }
}
```

☆ **TIP   Test Incrementally**

As you make each change, test the movie by pressing Ctrl-Enter (⌘⌘-Enter for Macintosh) on your keyboard. By testing the movie incrementally like this, you can fix small problems as they occur. If you wait until later, you'll have a harder time finding where you made an error.

Fine Tuning

At this point, everything should work okay, but the *Play* button looks identical to the *Stop* button. Add a layer to the main Timeline to identify each button. On this layer, place text over the corresponding buttons that reads "PLAY" and "STOP."

Maybe you want the animation to be stopped when the movie first loads. Add a *Tell Target* action to a keyframe to automatically stop the animation. You could type the action again from scratch, but since you've written it already, why not copy it?

While the *Stop* button is selected, you can copy the *Tell Target* and *Stop* actions from the text pane of the Actions panel. Select everything except for the `on (release)...` part and copy it. Then, select the keyframe and paste the copied action into the text pane of the Actions panel. You should see this in the text pane:

```
tellTarget("animate_me") {
    stop();
}
```

Other Things You Can Do with Tell Target

You can combine *Tell Target* with all kinds of actions and symbols. Some of these suggestions are somewhat advanced, but they are mentioned here to give you an idea of the power of *Tell Target*.

☆ Create a symbol with a sound track and turn the sound on and off. (Chapter Five explains this.)

☆ Create a more complex movie clip symbol with several different keyframes, or nest other movie clips within it. With a *Go To* action, this would allow it to be controlled in several ways. At a certain moment an action could call one keyframe on a character to lift its arm, another to grab something, and another to make a gesture.

☆ Add a second *Tell Target* action to the target clip itself. When the first *Tell Target* action sends an action to a second clip, a *Tell Target* action there could in turn target a third movie clip, like a chain reaction. You can use this strategy to create a sophisticated character animation or a clock. When a second hand movie clip on a clock gets to 60, it would send a *Tell Target* action to a minute hand clip, incrementing it.

☆ Use *Tell Target* to control a movie that was loaded with the *Load Movie* action. You could load a movie with an animation and let the user set its background color.

There are an infinite number of uses for *Tell Target*. The *Tell Target* action allows you to combine various symbols and actions. You could create a pretty elaborate interactive movie just with movie clips and *Tell Target* actions. There could be just one keyframe on the main Timeline, but a lot going on.

☆**WARNING**   **A Deprecated Action**

The *Tell Target* action is being deprecated, which means that future versions may not support it. If you publish a Flash SWF file on the Web that uses a deprecated action, be aware that it's possible that the action may not work with future versions of the Flash browser plug-in. For now, this will work on all browsers with a Flash plug-in, so there is no need for alarm.

You may wonder why a deprecated action such as *Tell Target* is included in this book at all. You can use ActionScript dot syntax in place of *Tell Target* (see Chapter Seven), but you risk compatibility problems with browsers that have plug-ins earlier than Flash 5. Presently, *Tell Target* is more compatible. Also, learning how to use *Tell Target* now will give you the background to learn ActionScript in Chapter Seven.

◎◎ Definining a Path

To apply the power of *Tell Target* to any object in your movie, you must understand how to assign different types of paths. Sometimes a path can be just the name of an instance, but a path can also describe a **hierarchy** when targeting objects within objects. The concept of paths can be challenging to understand at first; you may want to refer back to this section as you use the *Tell Target* action and begin to write ActionScripts in Chapter Seven.

Using the Target Path Window

The Target window can help you write a path. With the Target parameter selected in the actions panel, click on the Target icon and a window pops up (see Figure 4.7). This window will list any named movie clips instances in the current movie. Click on the clip that you want to target and Flash will write the path for you.

This feature doesn't always access every movie clip and it never accesses a loaded movie. In those cases, you still need to know how to write a path from scratch. The Target Path window is convenient, but learning how to write your own path now will help you with ActionScript later.

Relative Paths

A **relative path** describes the location of the target relative to the location of the action. You already know how to write a simple relative path. If the action is on the main Timeline and a target named *Tree* is on that same Timeline, then its relative path would be `Tree`.

Tell Target actions use **slash syntax** to find objects (i.e., movie clips) placed within other objects. A slash character separates the name of one object that's nested within another. In Figure 4.8, let's say you want to target the clip named *Apple* from a button or keyframe on the main Timeline. *Apple* is contained by a clip named *Tree*.

☆ From the main Timeline of the movie, the path `Tree` targets the tree clip.

☆ `Tree/Apple` targets *Apple* within *Tree*, one level deeper in the hierarchy.

☆ The relative path to a clip named *Seed* nested within the *Apple* clip would be `Tree/Apple/Seed`.

The / symbol between two instance names defines a path inside another clip object, and the `../` notation defines a path to the object that contains the current clip object. In Figure 4.8, the *Orange* clip is outside the *Tree* clip. If a *Tell Target* action is called from a keyframe (or button) inside the *Tree* clip to the *Orange*, its relative path would have to first lead up one level in the hierarchy from the *Tree* clip to the main Timeline.

☆ The path `../Orange` moves up one level to the main Timeline and targets the *Orange* clip there.

☆ From the Timeline of *Apple*, it would be `../../Orange`.

☆ In this case, the path `../` would target the main Timeline of the movie from the Timeline of *Tree*.

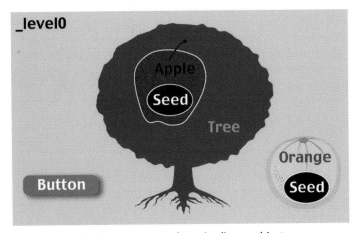

Figure 4.8 The relationships between nested movie clips or objects.

Absolute Paths

An **absolute path** ignores the location of the action and is based solely on where the target object (movie clip) is located. The absolute path to an object will not change unless the object itself moves. If the action is likely to move, but not the target clip, use the absolute path.

An absolute path can start with a slash or the key word _level0. Regardless of where it is called, the initial slash targets the main Timeline of the current movie. The path /`Tree` in Figure 4.8 would find the *Tree* clip whether it was targeted from inside the *Orange*, inside the *Apple*, or from the main Timeline.

The keyword *_level0* takes you to the main Timeline of whatever movie is loaded into Level 0. That refers to the same movie you are working on unless you have used the *Load Movie* action. If you have used the *Load Movie* action to load a second movie into Level 1, the absolute path to its Timeline would be `_level1` from either movie.

◎◎ Building a Pull-Down Menu

You can add a pull-down menu to a project as a way to conserve space. The menus at the top of the Flash program are similar to this. At rest, you see nine menus (File, Edit, View, etc.), but inside those are well over 100 commands to choose from. Here is how to create a simple version of this from within Flash.

The strategy is to first create a master symbol that opens the menu, revealing the individual menu buttons. From each menu button you can add *Tell Target* actions and other actions. Pull-down menus are opened either by a mouse rollover or by a click. This one uses a click.

Build the Master Menu Symbol

You can use the same file from the previous example for this. You need to build the main symbol that opens and closes the menu. Create a movie clip symbol with two keyframes: one for when the menu is hidden and one for when the menu is revealed.

Set Up the Closed View

☆ Create a new graphic symbol named *Menu* and label the keyframe *menu_closed*. This will be the closed view of the menu.

☆ Add a *Stop* action to the keyframe to prevent this symbol from playing inadvertently.

☆ Next, add an instance of a simple button symbol to the Stage. A one-frame button will do. It is better if this button doesn't respond visually to the mouse (i.e., have an *Over* or *Down* state).

☆ Add a *Go To* action with a *Release* mouse event to the button. Choose the *Go to and Stop* parameter. Select *Frame Label* as the Type and type *menu_open* in the Frame menu. This action will target the open view of the menu. You should see the following in the type pane:

```
on (rollOver) {
   gotoAndStop ("menu_open");
}
```

Set Up the Open View

☆ Insert a second keyframe to the Timeline of the *Menu* symbol and label it *menu_open*. This will automatically copy the button instance from the first keyframe with its actions. You'll soon see what a time saver this is.

☆ Add a *Stop* action to this keyframe to prevent the symbol from playing inadvertently.

☆ With the button from the second keyframe selected, go to the Actions panel. Notice that the actions from the button in the first keyframe are here. Change the Frame parameter to *menu_closed*. That's it!

This symbol will open and close the menu. The *Go To* action on the button in the *menu_closed* keyframe moves the movie to the *menu_open* keyframe; and the button in the *menu_open* keyframe moves it back to the *menu_closed* keyframe.

Create the Menu Items

Right now, the Stage for both the *menu_closed* and *menu_open* keyframes look identical. After the menu pops up (*menu_open*), it should reveal several options. It's time to add those options as secondary buttons, or menu items, to the *menu_open* keyframe.

☆ Create a button symbol named *Menu Item*. This button should react visually to the mouse (i.e., have an *Over* and *Down* state).

☆ Inside the Menu symbol, be sure that the *menu_open* keyframe is active. Place a few instances of the button symbol on the Stage and align them as in

Figure 4.9. Set them to *Track as Menu Item* from the Instance panel (Properties Inspector in Flash MX).

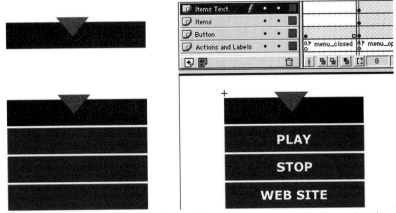

Figure 4.9 The closed and open versions of the same menu (left). The completed menu with its Stage and Timeline (right).

Hit Ctrl-Enter (⌘-Enter) for Macintosh) on your keyboard to test the menu thus far. The first time you click on the button, it should reveal the menu items (see Figure 4.10). Click the second time and it should hide them.

Assign Actions to the Menu Items

Assign an individual action to each menu button. To control something on the main movie, you'll use *Tell Target*. Use an absolute path (e.g., /animate_me) to target a clip on the main Timeline of the movie.

☆ To the first menu item, create a *Play* button as explained in the previous *Tell Target* exercise.

☆ To the second menu item, add a *Stop* button.

☆ To the other menu items, add links to your favorite Web sites with the *Get URL* action.

☆ To close the menu, append a *Go To* action to each button as well.

This is what you should see in the text pane for the Play button:

```
on (release) {
    tellTarget ("/animate_me") {
        play ();
    }
    gotoAndStop ("menu_closed");
}
```

Finish the *Menu* symbol by adding a layer with text labels. The labels should identify the menu items so that they look something like Figure 4.10. Check your work with Control→Test Movie.

☆ Summary

▷ You can add an action to a frame that will be triggered automatically, or add one to a symbol that someone can click on.

▷ All actions are applied by selecting a keyframe or object and working in the Actions panel.

▷ Flash provides several basic actions that allow you to add interactivity to a movie without knowing ActionScript.

▷ Various actions can stop or start the play of a movie, move it to a different frame, or link to any Web page.

▷ Combining actions with *Tell Target* and movie clip symbols allows you to create more complex interactions.

☆ Online References

Using JavaScript with *Get URL* Action
http://www.moock.org/webdesign/flash/launchwindow/
launchwindow-javascript.html

A Fun Example of *Tell Target* Actions with Movie Clips
http://www.pepworks.com/leosday.htm

Using Nested *Tell Target* Actions
http://www.macromedia.com/support/flash/interactivity/kscope/

Movie Clip Events
http://www.macromedia.com/support/flash/action_scripts/
actions/onclipevent.html

How to Use the Tell Target Action
http://www.macromedia.com/support/flash/ts/documents/
tell_target.htm

Example Paths
http://www.flashbible.com/members/TellTarget/Paths.htm

Using Load Movie
http://www.macromedia.com/support/flash/ts/documents/
loading_movie_clips.htm

Tell Target Diagram
http://www.flashbible.com/members/TellTarget/TTdiagram.htm

Creating Floating Button Labels
`http://www.flashkit.com/tutorials/Interactivity/`
`Creating-Eddie_Ca-60/index.shtml`

Using the fscommand to Control Display of Flash in Standalone Player
`http://www.macromedia.com/support/flash/ts/documents/`
`fscommand_projectors.htm`

☆ Review Questions

1. Describe the two types of events than can trigger an action.
2. Typically, how many frames does a button symbol have? How many layers?
3. How do you start and stop the playing of a movie?
4. How do you create a button so that it changes when a mouse rolls over it?
5. What action allows the movie to be played out of sequence?
6. How do you use Flash to link to a Web page?
7. Which action allows you to break up a Flash project into separate movies that play inside of a single main movie?
8. Describe two ways that a movie clip symbol differs from a graphic symbol.
9. What is the purpose of a *Tell Target* action? What must you do to a movie clip instance so that it can be a target?
10. In Figure 4.8, give two examples of the path from the seed within the apple to the seed within the orange. Give two examples of paths from the orange to the apple seed.

☆ Hands-On Exercises

1. In the new Flash file, create an animation on the main Timeline. Add an action to prevent it from playing past the first frame. Create a button symbol that looks depressed when clicked on. Assign an action to the button to make the movie play.
2. Place eight separate instances of a button on a page. Assign a *Play* action and a different mouse event on each button. Test the movie (Ctrl-Enter for Windows, ⌘-Enter for Macintosh) and try to trigger each button.
3. A navigation bar is a group of buttons that link to other pages on a Web site. Build a Flash navigation bar that links to 5 different pages on the same Web site.
4. Create a button that animates when the mouse rolls over it.
5. In the same Flash file, create a movie clip animation and place it on the Stage. Create another button that will start and stop that animation. Make the button work when the mouse hovers over it without clicking.

CHAPTER FIVE

ENRICHING MOVIES WITH SOUND

U p to this point we've focused on what you can see in Flash—words, pictures, and animations. Given what you already know, adding sound should not be too difficult to learn. Sounds add another dimension to your Flash movie. They can entertain visitors or compliment navigation. A short, well-placed sound effect or sound track can engage your audience deeper into a Flash movie and reinforce what is happening. Flash accepts sounds in various formats. And once they are in Flash, you can adjust them to work as you like.

◉◉ Chapter Objectives

☆ Understand the role of sound in Flash
☆ Import sounds and place them on the Timeline
☆ Modify audio settings for playback
☆ Optimize the download size and quality of sounds
☆ Control sounds with actions

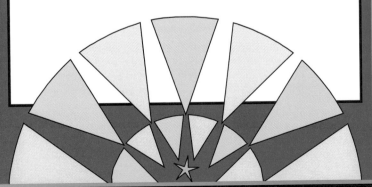

◎◎ When to Use Sound

If you combine sound with Flash's vector graphics, animation, and interactivity, you've got something much more compelling than HTML—and without expensive, hard-to-use software. Flash treats sound much like other objects, using the same Timeline that you should now be familiar with for creating animation and actions. You can mimic a click sound for a button, make a cartoon character's footstep sound real, or add a mood to a movie. Even without using its graphics features, you can use Flash to add sound to any Web page.

There are other techniques for adding sound to a Web page, such as Real Media, but they require specialized equipment or software. They are better suited for live Web broadcasting and lengthy video presentations. If you've already got Flash, you have enough to add sound to any Web site.

Use sounds appropriately in Flash. Sounds, especially the longer ones, add a lot of weight to a Flash movie's file size. They can make a good Flash movie more spirited or compelling, but there is a cost. Adding a big soundtrack to a navigation bar can annoy your audience and will add unnecessarily to the size of a Flash file. Apply a simple clack-clack sound to the movement of a character's feet and you can make your animation seem more real while adding little to the file size.

This chapter explains compression along with other strategies and tools for the efficient use of sound. Combine those tools effectively and you can enrich a Flash movie without a great impact on its file size.

◎◎ Importing Sounds Into Flash

Although it is not a program for creating original sounds, Flash allows you to import several popular formats of sound files. To use sound in Flash, you must either import a sound file or copy it from the library of another Flash document.

To import sounds, use File→Import command, just as you would for a bitmap image (see Chapter Two). When the import window pops open, select the sound you want and click the *Open* button (see Figure 5.1). From the Macintosh version of Flash 5, you'll have to first click the *Add* button to select one or more files and then the *Import* button.

☆**TIP**   **Are You Having Trouble Importing a Sound File?**

In some cases, the Flash program may have trouble recognizing a legitimate file. This can happen when you use a Macintosh version of Flash to open a file created in Windows or vice versa. If you don't see the file from the Import window and are sure that you can open it in Flash, choose *All Files* from the File Type menu. This will allow you to select any file on your computer. If it's a file that Flash can use, it will import without a hitch.

If a sound still will not import, you may need to install a QuickTime extension on your computer. Without the QuickTime extension (version 4 or later), Flash will not be able to import as many sound formats. If you don't have it or are unsure if you do, consult the Online References section at the end of this chapter.

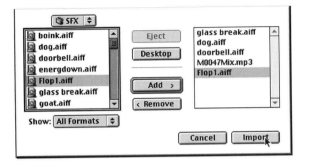

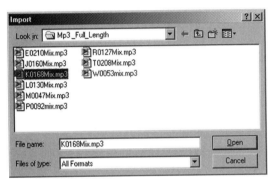

Figure 5.1 Two versions of the import menu for the Macintosh and Windows versions of Flash 5 (left). Sampling a sound from the library (right).

While selecting files from the File→Import window, use the menu labeled *Files of Type* (it's labeled *Show* for Macintosh). The default choice, *All Formats*, will show all files that can be imported into Flash. From that window, choose *All Sound Formats* to hide everything but sound files. If you're looking for a specific format, such as MP3 files, you can choose that filter (e.g., *MP3 Sound*).

Sources for Sounds

There are many sources for sound files. After you open another Flash file or library (File→Open as Library), just drag a sound file from that library to the library of the Flash file you are working on. You can purchase sound CD-ROMs from your favorite software source or download them from the Web. Look for sounds in the WAV, AIFF, or MP3 formats, which Flash supports. Check the Online Resources section at the end of this chapter for sites where you can download sounds.

☆ **SHORTCUT Try Out Sounds in the Common Libraries**

To follow along with these lessons, you don't necessarily need to comb the Web for sound files. The Flash program includes several sound files under Window→Common Libraries→Sounds. This isn't the most impressive sound collection, but it's convenient for learning.

Preparing Sounds for Flash

If you want to edit an actual sound file, you'll need to use a sound-editing program. If you aren't a sound pro, don't fret. You don't need to know any of these programs inside out to prepare existing sounds for Flash. You'll need them mostly just to edit the duration of sound files and save them. Check the Online Resources section at the end of this chapter for shareware and commercial programs available on the Web.

> ☆ **TIP   Avoid Stereo Sounds**
>
> If you use stereo sounds, they are double the file size of mono sounds. It's best to save them as mono. You'll see later in this chapter how to set stereo sounds to mono along with other compression settings in Flash.

Usually, Flash sounds don't require the highest quality settings. When saving a WAV or AIFF in another program, 16-bit mono sounds with a sample rate of 22kHz is a good general compression setting for Flash. For MP3 compression, a bit rate of 64kbps will give you decent quality and while keeping the file size modest. A setting as low as 16kbps might be acceptable for a sound, but you'll have to test the movie to hear for yourself. When in doubt, save a sound at a higher quality and recompress it later in Flash.

Managing Sounds in the Library

Like symbols and bitmap images, sounds are stored in a Flash document's library. You can change the name or delete a sound like any other asset in the library. You can also set its compression properties by double-clicking it. To sample a selected sound, click the triangular Play button in the preview window (see Figure 5.1).

It is all right to import more sounds than you need. Sounds in the library will not be exported as part of the final SWF file unless you place an instance on the Timeline of the movie. You can also delete any leftover sounds from the library.

◎◎ Placing a Sound on the Timeline

When you import a sound, it is added to the library, but not to the main movie. To play a sound in a movie, you must also assign an instance of it to the Timeline. You can assign a single instance of a sound to one keyframe or multiple instances to many keyframes.

To assign a sound, select a keyframe and apply a sound from the Sound panel. At the top of the Sound panel is a pop-up menu with the name of every sound in the current library. Choose a sound from that menu.

If you add sounds to multiple layers, you can play up to eight instances of sounds simultaneously. You can layer separate instances of the same sound or combine different sounds to create your own effects. However, overuse of this practice can lead to poor performance for users who play your final work on less powerful computers.

Like actions, sounds can be assigned to any keyframe in any layer on the Timeline. However, it's best for the sake of organization to create a dedicated sound layer. Add a sound to the Timeline of your movie and name it *Sounds*. If you want to play more than one sound at a time, then add another layer. As your work progresses, this will make it easier for you to access any sound placed in your movie.

☆ FLASH MX   Sound and the Properties Inspector

The Properties Inspector replaces the Sound panel in Flash MX. Select a keyframe and the sound options become available there (see Figure 5.2).

☆ SHORTCUT   Dragging Sounds from the Library

You can drag a sound directly from the library to a keyframe on the Timelime. This will apply the dragged sound to the keyframe.

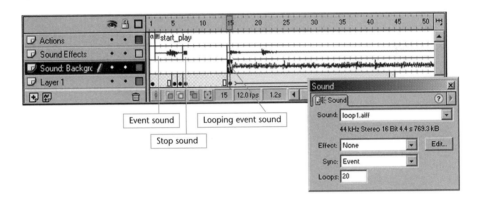

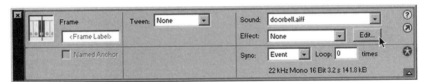

Figure 5.2 Assign sound instances to the Timeline via the Sound panel (top). In Flash MX use the Properties Inspector (bottom).

◎◉ Applying Playback Settings

Once you have assigned an instance of a sound to a keyframe, you can modify how it plays from the Sound panel (the Properties Inspector in Flash MX). These settings allow you to change the volume of a sound, make it repeat (loop), and specify how it will be triggered.

These settings do not alter the actual sound file; they only affect the playback of the sound. If you want to shorten the duration of a sound or change more than its volume level, you'll have to use a sound-editing program. See the Online

Resources section at the end of the chapter for links to commercial and shareware sound-editing programs.

Changing the Volume with the Effect Option

Use the Effect parameter to alter the volume of a sound instance. This menu offers several choices that have preset effects. You can create a fade-in or completely cut out the left channel. You can also use these settings to simulate stereo sound effects.

Choose the Custom option (or click on the Edit button) to reveal the *Edit Envelope* window. Here you will see a graphic representation of the sound, its **waveform** (see Figure 5.3). Click around in the window to move the handles and lines. They change the playback volume of the sound over its duration. Move the line down for the left channel to lower the volume in the left speaker on playback. Move the line up for the right channel to raise the volume in the right speaker on playback.

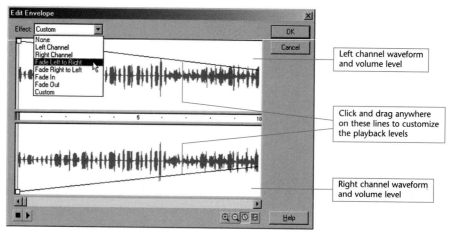

Figure 5.3 Changing a sound's playback levels.

Choosing a Sync Option

The *Sync* of a sound determines how it is triggered. Choose any setting for each instance of a sound. The four choices are explained below.

Sync Setting	Description
Event	The entire sound must download first before it can play. Once it is started, an *event* sound will play all the way through, even if the movie stops. You can trigger an *event* sound more than once and any extra instances will layer so that they play simultaneously.

Sync Setting	Description
Start	This is the same as *event*, except you cannot layer multiple instances of the same sound. Flash will only play a single instance of a *start* sound at once. If the first instance of a sound is still playing, a second instance triggered by a *start* sync will not play.
Stop	Stops the playing of a specified *event* or *start* sound.
Stream	Flash breaks up a *stream* sound into frame-sized pieces. Rather than waiting for an entire sound to download, each frame can play on its own.

A *stream* sound will also stop or start with the main Timeline of a movie, similar to the way a graphic symbol animation plays. You can use the *stream* setting to synchronize a sound to the motion of an animated character. However, this doesn't always work consistently. Depending on the speed of the computer a movie plays on, a *stream* sound may force the Timeline to skip the display of some frames to keep pace with it.

Setting a Loop Value

The *Loop* option allows you to continuously repeat the playing of a single instance of a sound. Rather than adding one enormous sound to your Flash movie, loop a much shorter sound. Use the loop setting in conjunction with the *event* or *start* sync. Enter a number to specify how many times a sound will repeat.

To use the loop feature, you should either find a pre-made sound loop or alter a sound in a sound-editing program. When preparing a loop sound, use your ear to make sure it repeats smoothly, so that it's not obvious where the end or the start of the sound is when it repeats. Test it out in Flash and see if it seems natural.

Flash has no setting to loop a sound forever, but you can specify the loop value as a very large number (100, 1000, or more) to achieve the same result. For a small file size, this would give you a long-playing sound. Place a *stop* sync of the same sound on the keyframe where you want it to stop playing.

☆WARNING **Avoid Looping Stream Sounds**

If you are using a sound more than once, or looping it, the *stream* sync is not the best setting. A *stream* sound downloads each time it is used. An *event* sound only downloads once no matter how many times it is used throughout the same movie. Use the *stream* sync only when you need a sound to synchronize with the Timeline or for larger sounds that will play only once.

◎◎ Maximizing Sound Compression

When you export a SWF file, its sounds are compressed according to a few settings. In applying these settings, the objective is to compress the sounds as much as possible without causing an unacceptable degradation (loss of quality) to the sound.

You can set the default compression for all of your sounds at once from File→Publish Settings (see Figure 6.6). The settings for Audio Event will apply to all sounds for a file except imported MP3 files. Check the *Override sound settings* option there to override the compression of every sound regardless of any individual settings. See Chapter Six for more about the Publish settings.

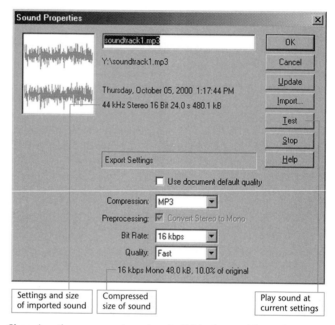

Figure 5.4 Changing the compression of an individual sound from the library.

If you take the time to set the compression separately for each sound (see Figure 5.4), you'll be able to get the optimal quality with the smallest file size. To specify the compression settings for an individual sound, select it in the library and choose the Properties option. (Or just double-click in the sound's icon in the library.) Change the *Compression* setting to something other than *Default*. (*Default* will apply the Publish Settings.) The changes you make here will apply to every instance of that sound.

As you change the compression of a sound, look at the bottom of the Properties window to verify the savings in file size. Also, click on the *Test* button to listen to the sound quality. The more you compress a sound, the more you will reduce the file size, but the more you will also degrade the quality of the sound. Experiment with different settings until you find a good balance between sound quality and file size. Simple sound effects can usually withstand a lot more compression than more complex or subtle sounds, but your ear is the best judge.

☆**WARNING** **No Unique Compression for Stream Sounds**

Unique sound settings are for sounds with *event* (and *start*) sync only. Changing an individual sound's compression will not apply when its *stream* is set to sync. All *stream* sounds are exported according to the Audio Stream settings from File→Publish Settings.

Using MP3 Compression

Flash works best with MP3 compression. Generally, it will give you better sound quality and smaller file sizes. If you import an MP3 format sound, Flash will retain its compression by default, much like an imported GIF or JPEG image.

The *Bit Rate* represents the amount of information saved for a sound and the *Quality* setting regulates how it is compressed. A lower bit rate (smaller number) will reduce the file size, but could also degrade the quality of the sound. A higher bit rate (greater number) will improve the quality of the sound but it will also increase the file size.

To optimize an MP3 sound:

☆ Start with *16 kbps* as the Bit Rate and *Fast* as the Quality.

☆ Test the sound and adjust the bit rate until you find an ideal setting.

☆ Leave the Quality set to *Fast* compression, which is appropriate for most Web projects.

☆ Always leave *Convert Stereo to Mono* checked. This will reduce the size of any imported stereo sounds by half.

When to Use ADPCM Compression

Short sound effects tend to perform better in this format. Also, MP3 compression won't work for Flash players (plug-ins) earlier than Flash 4, so you'll have to use this format if you want to support the widest possible audience.

The *Sample Rate* is the frequency of a sound wave. A higher setting here will reproduce a sound more accurately, but it adds to the overall file size. A setting too low here can cause a sound to distort or crackle. For Flash movies, a setting of 11kHz or 22kHz will usually work well. 44kHz is the standard for commercial CDs and is much higher in quality than is needed for the Web.

ADPCM Bits corresponds to the depth of information in the sound wave. A higher setting here allows for more subtle variations in the tone of the sound, but adds to the overall file size. If the setting is too low, the sound will be less clear.

To optimize a sound with ADPCM:

☆ Try 11kHz as the sample rate and 2 bit for ADPCM bits for short sound effects.

☆ If these settings degrade a sound too much, try increasing either setting. Some sounds may need to be set to 22kHz at 3 or 4 bit.

☆ Always leave *Convert Stereo to Mono* checked.

Controlling Sounds with Actions

◎◎ Adding Sound to a Button

Whenever a mouse rolls over it, not only can a button change its appearance, but it can also play a sound effect. When a user clicks on a button, it could make a "click" noise.

To add a sound effect to a button symbol, add a separate layer for sounds (see Figure 5.5). Insert one keyframe to the Over frame of that layer, and another to the Down frame. Then, assign a sound to each keyframe. The Over frame could have a more sublime sound effect to indicate that it is active; and the Down button could have a stronger sound to indicate the completion of a click.

This should make your Flash button seem more like a mechanical button. Place it in your movie as you would any other button. Then, assign an action to it. Click on the button and you'll hear a click sound.

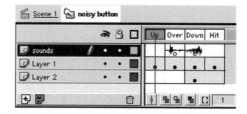

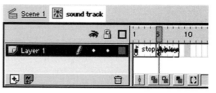

Figure 5.5 Button symbol with sound layer (top). Creating a soundtrack movie clip symbol (bottom).

◎◎ Controlling Sounds with Actions

Flash has a few actions that relate to sounds to help you control when a sound plays. Apply these to frames or buttons as you would any other actions. To use them, you must be familiar with how to create the actions in Chapter Four.

Stop All Sounds Action

An Event or Start sound will keep playing once it is started until it has played through completely. This is not an issue for a short sound effect, but for longer sounds or looped ones. Wherever you want to stop a specific sound from playing, add a *stop* sync to a keyframe.

There may be occasions where more than one sound plays at once. A movie may be designed to play this way automatically or a user may trigger an unknown number of sounds. Add the *Stop All Sounds* action to a keyframe or button where you want to ensure absolute silence.

☆ **FLASH MX**   **Using a Sound to Trigger an Action**

Now that sound is playing, and you want it all to be heard. Use the *onSoundComplete()* event handler to let the sound play through completely before triggering an action. Like any other event, a sound in Flash MX can move the movie to a different frame, transform an object, or even trigger another sound. A sound can play through and then present a menu of choices when it's finished, or it could start an animation. If you use this action to play another sound, then you could compose music by stringing snippets of individual sounds together, one after another. See your ActionScript reference for more information on this action.

Movie Clip Sounds and Tell Target

Chapter Four introduced *Tell Target* actions. The example presented there used *Tell Target* to control animation. Similarly, you can use a *Tell Target* action to play or stop a sound in a movie clip. This would allow you to add a soundtrack to the main Timeline of a movie, along with a button to stop or start it.

First create the movie clip with the sound:

☆ Create a movie clip symbol with two keyframes. It doesn't have to have any artwork.

☆ Add a *Stop* action to each keyframe.

☆ Assign the same sound in each of the two keyframes.

☆ In the first keyframe set the sync for the sound to *Stop*. This will stop the play of the sound.

☆ Set the sync to *Start* in the second keyframe and that will trigger it to play.

The Timeline should look something like the one at the bottom of Figure 5.5. You don't have to label the keyframes for the action to work, but if you do, it will help you identify what each keyframe does: a *stop_sound* frame and a *play_sound* frame. After it's complete, place an instance of this movie clip on the main Timeline and name it something like *soundtrack* so that it can be targeted by the *Tell Target* action.

Next, add a button to the Stage. This button will both start or stop the soundtrack. To this button, you'll add a *Tell Target* action nearly identical to what you used in Chapter Four. If you named the movie clip *soundtrack*, the following should appear in the text pane of the Actions panel:

```
on(release) {
    tellTarget("soundtrack") {
        play();
    }
}
```

Each click on the button tells the soundtrack movie clip to play. When the soundtrack plays, it advances to the next keyframe, where it triggers any actions and sounds. The first keyframe has an action to stop the movie clip and a sound sync to *stop* the sound from playing. The other keyframe stops the clip and *starts* the sound.

☆ **TIP**   **Pausing a Sound**

An *event* sound plays from start to finish every time it is called. However, a *stream* event sound is tied to a Timeline. Build a soundtrack movie clip with a *stream* sound and you can pause it with an action. You won't need any actions or labels in the Timeline of this clip, just enough frames to play the entire sound. Then use a *Tell Target* with a *Stop* action for a pause button. Create a play button the same way but with a *Play* action in place of the *Stop* action.

Loading Only the Sounds That Are Used

You can set up different soundtrack options in separate movies. This will free your users from having to download several large sounds if they only use one. First, create several one-frame movies that are blank with no artwork. Add a different soundtrack to the keyframe in each movie and export them as SWF files. Use File→Export to save SWF files. Keep track of their names (e.g., soundtrack1.swf, soundtrack2.swf, soundtrack3.swf).

Next, provide a menu or set of buttons with a choice of soundtracks. To each button, add a *Load Movie* action (see Chapter Four for more about the *Load Movie* action). You should see something like this in the text pane of the Actions panel for one button:

```
on(release) {
    loadMovieNum ("soundtrack3.swf", 10);
}
```

Want to take this further? You could set up each soundtrack with a movie clip as in the earlier *Tell Target* example. For each action that loads a movie, specify the same level number for each soundtrack choice (e.g., *10*). This would allow you to apply a universal play button that would play whatever soundtrack movie is loaded into level 10:

```
on(release) {
    tellTarget("_level10") {
        play();
    }
}
```

☆ **FLASH MX**   **The Load Sound Action**

With Flash MX, you can bypass loading entire movies. Use the *Load Sound* action to load MP3 files directly into a movie.

ActionScript Methods

If you get somewhat comfortable with ActionScript after completing Chapter Seven, there are several methods to access other parameters of a sound in a movie clip. You can change the volume or apply an effect from the *Edit Envelope* feature (explained earlier), but programmatically. Check out an ActionScript reference to see how to do this, and see the Online References section at the end of this chapter.

◎◎ Sound Strategy

Sounds can add the greatest weight to your file size. The easiest way to reduce the size of a Flash file is to remove sounds. Removing every sound will give you a smaller file, but possibly a less inspired Flash movie.

A better strategy is to be purposeful about using sounds. Consider why you are using a sound and what it adds to a movie. It's possible that your project would be just as compelling or better if it were silent. But when there's a good occasion for sound in your Flash movie, use it. A different sound for every button can annoy your audience and adds to the download time. But a short sound that gives a character a squeaky step can amuse your audience.

Chapter Six will go into depth about optimizing Flash movies. Following is a checklist for optimizing sound content in a Flash file:

☆ Like symbols, each sound is stored once in a file's library. Re-using the same sound in different places rather than using a different sound each time will save considerable file size.

☆ Loop shorter sounds in place of importing longer sounds.

☆ Compress sounds as much as they can stand without distorting them too much.

☆ If you use a separate sound-editing program, simplify each sound and remove extraneous noise.

☆ When you import sounds, try to pick the smaller ones if they work as well as the larger ones.

☆ Use an *If Frame is Loaded* action (see Chapter Six) to ensure that a sound is loaded before it should play.

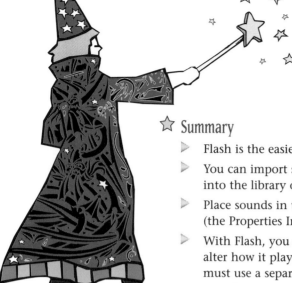

☆ Summary

▷ Flash is the easiest way to add sound to a Web page.

▷ You can import sounds saved in several popular formats into the library of a Flash movie.

▷ Place sounds in the main Timeline via the Sound panel (the Properties Inspector in Flash MX).

▷ With Flash, you can adjust several settings of a sound to alter how it plays and how it compresses. However, you must use a separate program to edit the duration of a sound.

▷ Add a sound to a button to give it another dimension.

▷ Use *Tell Target* and other actions to control when a sound is played.

▷ Sounds can add a lot to a Flash movie's file size. You can use sound to enhance a project, but use it purposefully.

☆ Online References

Installation Page for the QuickTime Extension
`http://www.apple.com/quicktime/download`

Smart Sound Editor with Sounds
`http://www.smartsound.com/fm`

SoundForge Sound Editor for Windows
`http://www.sonicfoundry.com/products/NewShowProduct.asp?PID=460`

Studio Sound Shareware Sound Editor for Macintosh
`http://www.felttip.com/products/soundstudio`

Cool Edit Shareware Sound Editor for Windows
`http://www.syntrillium.com/cooledit`

FlashKit Public Domain Sounds
`http://www.flashkit.com/soundfx`
`http://www.flashkit.com/loops`

The Sound Effects Library
`http://www.sound-effects-library.com`

Killersound Store
`http://www.killersound.com`

Find Sounds by Category
`http://www.stonewashed.net`

Remixology Audio Column
`http://www.sonify.org/home/feature/remixology`

Using Sound Methods to Build Sound Controls (requires ActionScript)
`http://f256.com/comm/articles/flash/`
`sound_objects-introduction.asp`

Going All Out with Sound and ActionScript
`http://showstudio.com/projects/031/031_interactive.html`
`http://www.amontobin.com`

☆ Review Questions

1. Where do you store a sound and change its compression settings?

2. Why should you avoid using stereo sounds in Flash?

3. Where do you place a sound in a movie?

4. Explain the difference between an *event* and a *stream* sound.

5. List two ways to make a sound stop playing.

6. Describe an example in which you would use a *stream* sound sync.

7. To maximize sound compression, what two factors must you balance?

8. Which sound compression format in Flash usually gives you the best general quality *and* compression?

9. Which type of compression can work well for short, simple sound effects?

10. List three ways to use sound more efficiently in Flash.

☆ Hands-On Exercises

1. Open the file you used to create a motion tween for Chapter Three. Import a sound file. Add a sound layer to the Timeline of the movie and apply a sound effect that starts at the same frame as the animation. The sound should somehow relate to the animation. For example, a bouncing ball could make a bounce sound.

2. Building on Exercise 1, insert a keyframe with a *Stop* action before the animation starts. To the same keyframe add a short sound event loop that will continue to play through a long wait. Add a play button to start the animation on the main Timeline. The soundtrack should stop when the animation begins.

3. Import a large sound file and set its compression in the library to MP3, with a bit rate of 8kbps. Test the file. Change the bit rate to 64kbps and test again. Pay attention to sound quality and file size in both cases. Try it with ADPCM compression too. Which compression is better and why?

4. Create a button symbol that makes a sound when the mouse rolls over it or clicks it.

5. Create a movie clip soundtrack. Place stop and start buttons to control the soundtrack with *Tell Target* actions.

OPTIMIZING AND PUBLISHING

Y ou should now have the foundation to create some pretty sophisticated Flash movies with animation, sound, and basic interactivity. Why not put it on the Web? Well, there's more work involved than just saving a file. This chapter focuses on publishing Flash movies and provides some strategies for optimizing your work to improve its performance.

Chapter Objectives

☆ Optimize Flash files to export smaller movies that download faster and display more quickly

☆ Use the Movie Explorer to analyze and navigate the content of your files

☆ Use the Bandwidth Profiler to find bottlenecks and simulate how a Flash movie will load in the real world

☆ Build a loading sequence to ensure the smooth playing of a movie

☆ Export SWF files and embed them into Web pages

☆ Learn what it takes to publish content that's compatible for everyone

◎◎ Optimizing Flash Content

You put a lot of work into your Flash project, so you probably want people to be able to check it out. If someone has to wait forever to see your Flash masterpiece, at the least they'll get annoyed and they'll probably give up and check out another Web site. Here are a few strategies for creating Flash files that can be delivered efficiently to your audience.

Minimizing File Size and Maximizing Bandwith

A Web site is a collection of files with text, images, and sounds. When someone opens a page in their Web browser, these files must transmit through the Internet to their computer. Roughly, the larger the file size, the longer the page will take to display. Flash files are no exception.

Bandwidth is often used as a synonym for file size. More specifically, it's the amount of information that transmits to a Web browser over time. The two main factors that govern bandwidth are the speed of the Internet and the size of files. Increasing the speed or reducing the file size improves the bandwidth, resulting in Web pages that display more quickly.

The speed of the Internet for your audience will vary. Some people use cutting-edge computers at their jobs that have blazing fast connections. Others browse at home with old dial-up modems and hand-me-down computers. Network traffic is another factor. On days with heavy Internet traffic, even the fastest connection can take as long as the old modem.

You can't change the speed of the Internet, but you can control the file size of your Flash movies. File size is measured in kilo*bytes* (KB). The speediest Internet connection could download a 600KB file in a few seconds, but with a slow modem it would take several minutes. Cut that 600KB to 60KB and you'll reduce the download to one-tenth the time. Most modems download at a rate of 2–5KB per second. Keep that audience in mind to ensure a good experience for everyone. As you work, you can follow a few strategies to keep your files as trim as possible.

Use Symbols and Keyframes Strategically

Symbols and keyframes are two of your biggest allies in keeping file size down. (Chapter Three goes into detail about the virtues of symbols.) Several symbol instances in a movie add much less to file size than separate non-symbol objects, so build your movies by reusing symbol components.

Each individual object in a Flash file adds to its size. Let's say you draw a tree. Each frame where that tree appears would normally contain all of the information to display a tree. If that tree were a symbol, it would instead exist just once in the library. Every time a tree would appear in the movie there would be an instance with no information about how to display the tree. Instead, each instance would reference the original symbol in the library which would have that information. You could create a forest of trees from one symbol (see Figure 6.1).

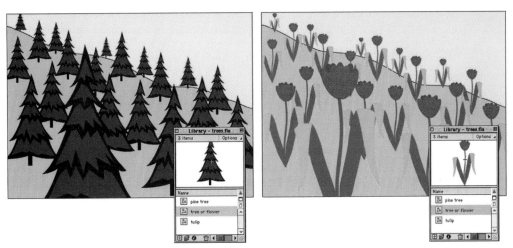

Figure 6.1 From one symbol, you can create a forest of trees, or change them all at once to tulips.

The more keyframes with changes, the larger your file would be. However, keyframes with fewer or smaller objects add less to the file size than keyframes with every last object in a scene. Use multiple layers to separate the moving parts of an animation from the static parts that don't change (see Figure 6.2).

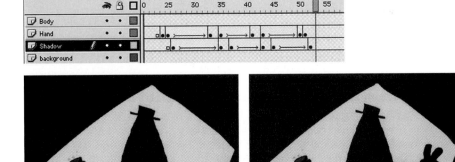

Figure 6.2 The only thing that needs to animate here is the hand of the character and the hand of its shadow. [Mr. Man in Shadow by Steve Whitehouse is presented by AnimationExpress.com]

Minimize the Use of Bitmap Images and Sound

No matter how efficient your Flash skills are, the more bitmap images and sounds you add to a Flash movie, the larger the file will be. Don't overuse them. When practical, create original artwork as vector images. Try the Modify→Trace Bitmap command to convert simpler bitmap images into vector art and see if that helps. (For more complex images, it may add to the file size.) Sounds are a compelling feature in Flash, but they also add a lot of weight to file size. Don't avoid them, but be aware that every sound or bitmap image you add to a movie impacts its performance.

Like symbols, bitmap images and sounds are stored in the library. If you are using a sound or bitmap image once in your movie, feel free to use it multiple times. Reuse a sound in different places rather than importing lots of different ones; loop a shorter sound file instead of importing a larger file. Multiple instances of the same bitmap image or sound would not add much to the file size, but using several different ones would.

Utilize Compression Settings

Whether you are using few sounds and images or many, you should take advantage of compression. There are two ways to set compression: for the entire movie or for a single asset. In File→Publish Settings (covered later in this chapter), you can specify the default compression for every sound and bitmap image in a movie. In the library, use the *Properties* option to override the compression for a selected bitmap image or sound asset.

It's better to compress a bitmap image outside of Flash in a program such as Adobe ImageReady or Macromedia Fireworks since they provide better optimization controls. You'll get the best results if you save an image at the same size it will display within the Flash movie. Every GIF, JPEG, or PNG image that you import into a Flash movie retains its own compression settings by default. The compression of an imported GIF or PNG image should be set to *Lossless (PNG/GIF)*. JPEG images should be set to *Photo (JPEG)* with *Use imported JPEG data* checked.

Other image formats are compressed within Flash. By default, a movie's JPEG compression will apply to them. From File→Publish Settings, try the *JPEG Quality* at 40 and see if the bitmap images still look acceptable when you test a movie. If not, try a higher value. To really conserve file size, you can try a setting of 30 or lower. You can also set the compression for these images individually from the library.

The compression of sounds, except imported MP3 files, is ruled by Flash and overrides whatever compression they had before they were imported. MP3 compression is the best general setting, but there are exceptions. If you take the time to individually set the compression of each sound in the library, you can minimize file size and maximize quality. Chapter Five addresses sound compression in more detail.

Optimize Vector Graphics

Vector images are usually very kind to file size. But if you create a very complex graphic with lots of corners and intricate details, it can defeat the savings. Remove stray lines and shapes; and use Modify→Optimize to streamline a selected vector object.

Prioritize the Content

There is no exact number you could point to as an ideal size for a SWF file, but each kilobyte is a precious chunk of bandwidth. There are trade-offs: an extra 10KB for a sound effect in one place can be compensated for by removing a 10KB image somewhere else. Including both would result in a larger Flash movie, so it should be worth the extra download.

An ad banner directed toward business people shouldn't take more than a few seconds to load. A singing animated greeting card for a loved one could take a while longer since its audience would be more patient. Consider each sound, bitmap image, or other weighty object and decide if it's worth the size that it adds to the file.

Speeding Up the Display

File size is only part of the equation for performance in Flash. A movie may download all right, but it still may not animate smoothly. This depends on how you build the movie and how well a user's computer can **render** (display) it. You have no control over your audience's equipment, but you can look out for elements in a file that might cause rendering problems.

Flash has no automatic feature for testing display speed, but you can check it on your own. First use Control→Test Movie to observe how a movie renders. Also, publish a SWF file and try it out on a slower computer. See "Testing in a Web Browser" later in this chapter for more details. Depending on how they are used, the following can cause rendering problems:

☆ Gradient fills (radial gradients are worse)

☆ Alpha transparency effect

☆ Masks

☆ Intricate vector artwork

☆ Large bitmap images

☆ Long blocks of text

☆ Layering or animating any of the above

☆ A movie with very large dimensions

☆ Complex ActionScript

The size of the area that changes has a bearing on all of this. Small areas of change can render quickly, but large areas that change every frame can cause rendering problems. Each time something changes on the Stage, the Flash player (browser plug-in) and the computer are hard at work re-drawing the area that changes. Sometimes the change overwhelms this process, causing the movie to halt temporarily or play erratically.

You don't need to avoid any of the techniques listed above, but you should moderate their use and take note of them during testing. If you see a rendering problem in the movie that coincides a large gradient fill image animating across the Stage, you may want to change that gradient fill to a standard fill or simplify the animation.

Taking Advantage of Streaming

A Flash file can play while it is still downloading. You could publish a relatively large Flash movie and no one would know the difference. This sleight-of-hand feature is called **streaming**. The movie will keep loading while your audience is occupied reading, watching, or playing with something. If someone is looking at something on Frame 12 while Frame 80 is downloading, the download would seem nonexistent.

A Flash movie downloads from the first frame forward. Once a frame has been loaded, it can play. When a movie pauses or plays frames with less going on, it continues to download successive frames that haven't yet played. Use the Bandwidth Profiler with the Show Streaming option (explained later in this chapter) to simulate this.

To take advantage of streaming, set up the beginning of your movie with no sounds or large images. The movie should start with lightweight distractions. A *Stop* action halts the play of the movie while a user makes a choice, but the movie continues to download invisibly. Text might be appropriate here to introduce or explain the Flash movie. A very streamlined animation at the beginning will allow a large sound or bitmap image in a later frame to load in the background. A loading loop (covered later) can help too.

◎ The Movie Explorer

The Movie Explorer can help you find any object placed in a Flash movie. Use it to find a symbol instance, text, or script, or to analyze the entire architecture of the movie.

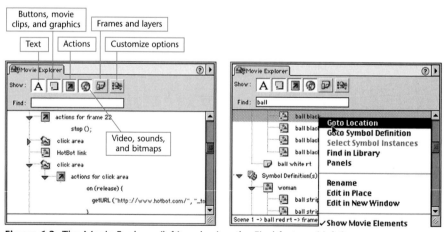

Figure 6.3 The Movie Explorer (left) and using the Find feature (right).

The Movie Explorer's main window represents the Flash movie in an outline format. Double-click on an object to jump to it on the Stage and Timeline. Right-click (Ctrl-click for Macintosh) on a listed object to reveal a contextual menu for other options (see Figure 6.3).

There are several buttons at the top of the Movie Explorer panel. Click them to hide or reveal text, symbols, actions, bitmaps, sounds, and frames. If you are looking only for actions, then leave just that button depressed.

If you are looking for a specific symbol, frame label, or some text, you can search for it from the *Find* box. Type what you are searching for there and press the Enter key on your keyboard. If you are searching for every instance of a symbol with the word "ball" in it, type that in the *Find* box (see Figure 6.3). The main window in the Movie Explorer will reveal only objects that contain the word "ball."

☆ **TIP   A Confusing Search**

The Movie Explorer has a flaw that may confuse you at first. When you use the find feature, the Movie Explorer shows what you are searching for. That's what it should do, but it doesn't give you an obvious way to reveal everything again after your search. To do this, delete whatever is in the *Find* box and press the Enter key on your keyboard.

◎◎ Testing Movies with the Bandwidth Profiler

From previous chapters, you should already be familiar with using Control→Test Movie to preview your movie. This feature saves a temporary SWF file, the same as what you would publish on a Web site. It is an accurate way to check if your actions and movie clips behave as they should.

From the Test Movie window, you can reveal the Bandwidth Profiler, a Timeline graph for analyzing how a movie would download and play on the Web. The Bandwidth Profiler also provides detailed file-size information about the SWF file, and allows you to simulate how it streams. If it doesn't appear (see Figure 6.4) when you test a movie, choose View→Bandwidth Profiler.

While you are testing a movie, do the following:

☆ Look at the way the movie streams. Are there any awkward pauses? Try it with a few different speeds from the Debug menu.

☆ Check the overall file size.

☆ Make sure the animations work the way you intended them to.

☆ Check to see if the quality of the images and sounds is acceptable.

☆ Try every action in as many different ways as possible.

☆ Review error messages or anything else that appears in the Output window.

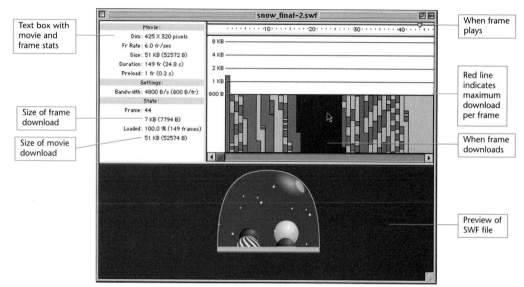

Figure 6.4   Test Movie preview with Bandwidth Profiler.

Connection Speed

Under the Debug menu, you can select from different connection speeds (e.g., 28.8, 56K) to compare how a file will load for different users. You can set faster rates under the Debug→Customize option.

The slower rates tend to be more meaningful because anything that downloads on a slower connection will also play well over a faster connection. If your movie plays smoothly at the 28.8 speed, chances are that almost everyone will have a good experience. If it only plays well at a cable modem speed, then anyone with a slower Internet connection will not have as good an experience.

The speeds listed are idealized, but not always accurate in the real world. Most people in the United States have a 56K or faster connection, but Web traffic at certain times can reduce that. Users in most other countries tend to have more problems due to slower networks. If you optimize for 56K, most people will see the movie play all right, but you should also pay attention to the 28.8 speed to make sure the slower speed is acceptable.

Reading the Timeline Graph

The Timeline graph will change to reflect the speed you choose. It is a graphical representation of the way your movie should play and download at the selected connection speed. The text box to the left displays the size of the current SWF file and whichever frame is visible (see Figure 6.4).

Each gray box on the Timeline graph represents a frame as it downloads. The frame indicator at the top signifies which frame is playing. Remember streaming from the previous section? If View→Streaming Graph is selected, each gray box is placed on the graph according to when it should download at the selected connection speed. Click on a gray box and the playhead will move to the corresponding frame where that content will play. Usually, it's a different frame than where it loads, indicating that the frame will load before it plays.

The gray box for frame 20 may sit under the indicator for frame 16. This means that frame 20 should be downloaded by frame 16, and ready to be displayed before the playhead crosses frame 20. If the gray box rises above the red line at frame 20, then the movie will likely pause just before frame 20 while it finishes downloading its contents. The higher it rises above that line, the longer the movie will lag.

Every frame is a different size according to its contents. If it has no keyframes, the corresponding gray box will be very small. If it's got a heavy sound or bitmap image, it will be larger. If there are enough lightweight frames between the heavier ones, the movie will tend to play through smoothly. It's acceptable for the first frame to rise slightly above the red line, but you should prevent the download from lagging after that.

Show Streaming

Choose View→Show Streaming to simulate how the movie will play. It is based on the current speed selected under the Debug menu. The animation will play in the preview area while the Timeline graph progresses. The frame indicator points to which frame is playing, while color shading highlights the download progress. Look at both the preview and the graph, and repeat the Show Streaming command a few times to get a better idea of how a movie will load over a slower modem. If it is likely to pause on a modem, it will pause here.

Smoothing the Stream

You could ignore the bottlenecks in your movie and it won't be broken, but it would halt at awkward places. It's better to fix those bottlenecks. Here are a few strategies:

☆ Think minimal. Streamline the graphics, symbols, and sounds as discussed earlier in this chapter in the section "Optimizing Flash Content." Remove some if possible.

☆ Simplify the frames with the largest gray bars in the Bandwidth Profiler, especially the ones that rise above the red line (see Figure 6.4).

☆ Change the compression settings for the entire movie or for the largest images and sounds.

☆ Reorder content or extend the first part of the movie. This can give the later parts of the movie more time to download.

☆ Pace the download. Rather than placing the meat of the movie up front, design the movie so that those larger sound files and bitmap images can download one at a time.

☆ If the movie will not play smoothly otherwise, add a loading sequence at the beginning.

◎◎ Creating a Loading Loop

Flash movies download from the first frame toward the last frame. As soon as the first frame has been loaded, it can play in the Web browser. As soon as the second frame is loaded, it will play, and so on. Sometimes there may be a bottleneck where there's too much to download in a single frame. The movie will pause awkwardly at a frame like this until the download is complete.

If your movie is just too large to play smoothly otherwise, you can pre-load enough to make sure it does. When your movie arrives at that animation and sound effect in frame 80, you may want to be sure that frame is already loaded, preventing a delay. You can use the *If Frame is Loaded* action to check if frame 80 has been downloaded. Like a mouse event handler, *If Frame is Loaded* does nothing by itself. Append a *Play* action to it, and it will check to see how much of the movie has been loaded before it plays.

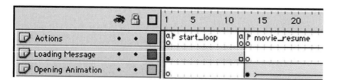

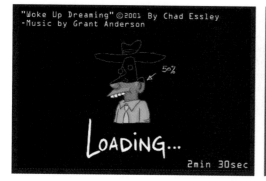 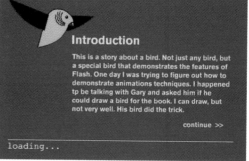

Figure 6.5 Two examples of a pre-loader message and an example Timeline of a loading loop. ["Woke Up Dreaming" by Chad Essley is presented by AnimationExpress.com]

A popular way to use *If Frame is Loaded* is for a *loading* phase in a Flash movie (also called a *pre-loader*). The more you pre-load at the start, the smoother the Flash movie will tend to play. Force the movie to wait until the bulk of it is loaded, and it will play through without a hitch. This strategy combines a few basic actions from Chapter Four and introduces a new one.

☆ Set aside a few frames at the start of the movie for the loading section that will play over and over until the designated frame is loaded.

☆ Label the first keyframe in this section something like *start_loop*.

☆ Add a second keyframe at the end of the loading section with a *Go To* action. Assign `start_loop` as the Frame parameter. You should see this in the text pane:

```
gotoAndPlay ("start_loop");
```

This completes the wait loop. As it is, the movie will replay those first frames forever. Next, you will add the *If Frame is Loaded* action to take the movie out of the loop.

☆ Insert a third keyframe just after the second one that will mark the start of where the movie resumes playing. This is just after the loading section. Label it something like *movie_resume*.

☆ Add the *If Frame is Loaded* action to the first keyframe. On the Actions panel, you'll find it under Basic Actions for Flash 5 or under Deprecated→Actions for Flash MX.

☆ Enter a frame number (e.g., 80) for the Frame parameter. Then, add a *Go To* action just below that. Choose *Frame Label* for the Type parameter and *movie_resume* for the Frame parameter. This is what you should see in the text pane:

```
ifFrameLoaded (80) {
    gotoAndPlay ("movie_resume");
}
```

Each time the loop plays, the *If Frame is Loaded* action will check to see if everything up to frame 80 (or whatever frame you entered) has been loaded. If it hasn't, Flash will ignore the *Go To* action and play through the wait loop. If it *has* been loaded, the movie will jump out of the loop to the frame labeled *movie_resume* and continue playing from there.

Once you have set up these keyframes, you can go to the Stage and compose what will display during the loading loop. You could create a simple "loading..." message, or give your audience something more substantial to read or entertaining to watch (see Figure 6.5).

☆**WARNING** **A Deprecated Action**

Flash 5 and Flash MX both support the *If Frame is Loaded* action, but it is being deprecated, which means that future versions may not support it. If you publish SWF files using a deprecated action and forget about it, it's possible that the action may not work with future versions of the Flash browser plug-in. However, this is a good introduction to **conditional statements**, which will be covered in Chapter Seven.

You can achieve the same results working directly with ActionScript, but you may risk compatibility problems with browsers that have older Flash 3 plug-ins. *If Frame is Loaded* is compatible with the older plug-in and easier to implement if you don't know ActionScript. For now, it will work on all browsers with a Flash plug-in.

◉◎ Publishing Flash Content for the Web

Flash is primarily for the Web, so you'll likely want to add it to a Web page. This requires two basic things:

☆ Export a SWF file.

☆ Create HTML to **embed** (contain) the file.

The Publish feature can create everything you need to publish Flash on the Web. It exports a SWF file and can automatically generate the HTML to embed the file in a Web page.

To get the most from this feature, choose File→Publish Settings, not File→Publish. At the top of this window are a few tabs (see Figure 6.6). Each tab loads specific parameters that allow you to optimize the SWF file and HTML code for your needs. You can export everything you need once you've set the options here. From this window, there are four buttons available at the right:

☆ OK: Closes the Publish window and saves the current Publish settings. This doesn't export any files. The current Publish settings will be retained for the current work file. They will also apply if you subsequently use the File→Export or Control→Test Movie command.

☆ Publish: Exports at once all of the files you have checked on the Formats menu. After you have reviewed the settings and wish to publish content, click this button.

☆ Cancel: Saves nothing and returns to the Flash movie.

☆ Help: Opens detailed information about the Publish settings.

Click on the *Formats* tab to select the file formats you want to publish. At minimum, you should check Flash and HTML. The Publish feature will save the selected files as they are named here. After checking the formats, click on the corresponding tabs to adjust the settings for the Flash movie, the HTML page, and any other formats you have chosen. When you are done, click the Publish button to export every file at once. Then click OK to return to editing the movie.

☆WARNING **Naming File Conventions**

Flash will let you name the SWF files whatever you want, but the Web is less forgiving. Use only alphanumeric characters (a-z and 0-9). Separate those characters with a dash (-) or underscore (_), if needed for clarity. You may use both capital and lowercase letters, but never use spaces. The file must end with *.swf* to be recognized properly by Web browsers. Format it like this: *sunny_day3.swf*, not this: *sunny day 3*. It's not required, but it is good practice to follow the same guidelines for the Flash work files, except that their names should end with the *.fla* extension (e.g., *sunny_day.fla*).

☆ **FLASH MX**   **Shortcut to Publish Settings**

When there is nothing selected, the Properties Inspector offers a Publish button. Click the button adjacent to the word *Publish* to go directly to the Publish settings.

Publishing Flash Content for the Web

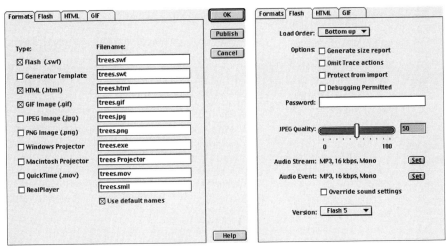

Figure 6.6 The Formats and Flash settings for the Publish feature.

Flash Movie Settings (for the SWF file)

Click on the Flash tab to modify general settings for the actual SWF file. You don't need to tinker too much with these parameters. The defaults will work well in most cases.

Parameter	Description
Load Order	Applies to the layers you used to create the Flash file. Flash will render (display) the movie starting with the bottom layer by default. You can force it to load starting from the top layer instead.
Generate size report	Saves a text file that details the size of individual elements in your file. It's for those who crave more information than the Bandwidth Profiler provides.
Omit Trace actions	Allows you to remove extraneous *Trace* actions from ActionScript to reduce file size. Covered in Chapter Seven, the *trace()* function is used for debugging purposes only. This option is a must if you use the *trace()* function copiously.
Protect from import	Prevents others from using the Flash program to open the SWF file. However, this isn't fool-proof since there are other programs that can open files saved this way.
JPEG Quality	Determines the default compression of bitmap images in your Flash movie. It will not override the settings of an imported JPEG, GIF, or PNG image.

continues

Parameter	Description
Audio Stream	Determines the default compression of sounds that are triggered by the *Stream* sync.
Audio Event	Determines the default compression of sounds that are triggered by the *Event* or *Start* sync.
Override sound settings	Overrides the compression of all sounds in the library, regardless of any individual settings, and applies the movie's default setting to them. This will also override the compression of any imported MP3 files.
Version	Allows you to save a Flash file that's compatible with an older Flash plug-in (player). The player for Flash MX content is called *Flash 6*.

☆ **FLASH MX**   Compress Movie

Why not? Anything to conserve file size. This parameter can reduce the file size of Flash movies with lots of ActionScript or text. But it's only for movies to be played with a Flash 6 player.

☆ **SHORTCUT** Exporting a SWF File with File→Export Movie

As an alternative, File→Export Movie will save the same SWF movie as the Publish feature does but only the SWF file. After you choose this command, a window pops up. Choose *Flash Player* as the format. (The other choices allow you to export your file for other programs.) Name the file and click the *Save* button. After that, a menu will pop up with various choices for optimizing the Flash movie. These are the same options as the Publish Movie Settings above. Click OK when done.

HTML Settings

This window (from the HTML tab) relates to the HTML file that embeds the Flash SWF file. The default settings here will work in many cases, but you can choose what is right for your project. Flash will generate an HTML file based on what you choose here (see Figure 6.7).

Parameter	Description
Dimensions	Sizes the movie exactly as created when *Match Movie* is chosen. Choose other options to resize it larger or smaller.
Playback: Paused At Start	Prevents the movie from playing past the first frame when loaded.
Playback: Display Menu	Allows your users to right-click ([Ctrl]-click for Macintosh) on a Flash movie to reveal a menu of play options.

Parameter	Description
Playback: Loop	Allows the movie to play over and over again. In most cases, uncheck it to prevent movie from replaying.
Playback: Device Font	Replaces embedded fonts with fonts on the user's system. Leave this unchecked.
Quality	Determines how the Flash movie will display. The default is high, and that's what you should choose in most cases. If you experience awkward pauses in the display, you can try other settings. However, it's best to redesign the problematic part of the movie to play better than to compromise the display quality.
Window Mode	Allows you to overlay Flash content with HTML content. This only works for Windows Internet Explorer, so it's not a reliable feature.
HTML Alignment	Affects the alignment of the Flash movie within the Web page.
Scale	Determines how the Flash movie will be resized if the Dimensions have been changed.
Flash Alignment	Determines how the movie will be positioned within the dimensions specified if the Dimensions setting has been changed.

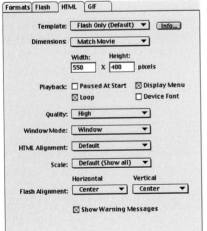 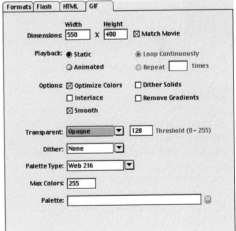

Figure 6.7 The HTML and GIF settings for the Publish feature.

HTML Templates

The Publish feature saves HTML pages that are formatted based on various templates. The Template option at the top of the HTML Publish settings allows you to choose from several different formats depending on your needs. You can generate a simple page with basic embed tags or one that uses JavaScript to detect for the proper Flash plug-in.

Flash Only

The Default setting is *Flash Only*. This will create basic code to embed a Flash movie for all browsers that have the plug-in installed. It also supports the ActiveX control built into Windows Internet Explorer browsers. This is the appropriate template if you can count on your users having the right plug-in, but it can be a problem for those who don't have it.

If you publish the HTML as *Flash Only*, someone without a Flash plug-in would get a warning message and see a broken icon instead (see Figure 6.8). Those with an older version of the plug-in may be baffled by a blank area where the Flash movie belongs, or by a movie that doesn't function correctly.

Figure 6.8 A Web page with no Flash plug-in (left). A page with an outdated plug-in (right).

Detecting for a Plug-in

The ideal setup is to serve different content based on what the user can support. If someone has an older version of Flash, you could export an alternate version of your movie that's compatible with that. For users who don't support Flash at all, you could serve them a GIF or JPEG image, which all browsers support. Even if you decide that your Web site will require the latest version of the Flash plug-in, you should alert those who don't have it what they need to do: download the latest version of the plug-in.

The *Ad 5 Banner* template will generate a Web page that uses JavaScript to detect for a Flash 5 plug-in. (The name of this template is a bit of a misnomer because it's not just for ad banners.) Use this feature with *GIF* or *JPEG* selected from the Format window, and whoever doesn't have the Flash 5 plug-in will see a bitmap image instead.

The *Ad 3 Banner* and *Ad 4 Banner* templates work the same way except that they require the Flash plug-in be at least version 3 or 4 respectively. For more about working with older plug-ins see the "Accommodating Older Plug-ins" section later in this chapter.

☆ **FLASH MX   New HTML Templates**

Flash MX has renamed the *Ad 5 Banner* template as *Detect for Flash 5*, and others similarly. It's the same template, but named more generically.

These templates ensure that everyone gets something, even if they don't have the proper Flash plug-in installed. They will get less than they would with the appropriate plug-in, but they won't necessarily notice that anything is broken.

☆ **WARNING   Embedding with JavaScript and Netscape 4**

The JavaScript created by these templates can cause problems with certain layouts on the Netscape 4 browser. This can happen when you insert this code into an HTML table, especially if that table is nested within another table. It doesn't occur in every case, so you'll have to test it out with that browser to see if it's all right.

Customizing Templates

If you love tinkering with code and you aren't satisfied with the templates that are included with the Flash program, you can change them to suit your needs. You could, for example, create a template that serves different Flash SWF files depending on which plug-in is installed. Or, you could format a template that generates a complete Web page that's formatted specifically for your site. The *Templates* option refers to actual template files installed on your computer.

In Flash 5, you should be able to find the templates wherever the Flash program is installed. In Flash MX, their location depends on your computer's operating system. (For Windows look within a folder named *Application Data*, and for Macintosh OS X look within a folder named *Application Support*.) Located with other Flash-related items, you will find a folder named *HTML* that contains these template files. With any text-editing program, you can open and modify these templates, copy them, or save new ones. For details, search for "Customizing HTML publishing templates" from Flash's help feature.

Alternative Formats

Naturally, Flash is the most efficient and best quality format for Flash content. Other formats are available to export non-Flash content. Select the formats you want under the Formats tab from File→Publish Settings.

GIF or JPEG

For the plug-in detection described earlier, you can export a JPEG or GIF image of your Flash movie. Depending on which image type you choose, settings will become available for compressing the bitmap image.

QuickTime

Flash allows you to import a QuickTime video as you would any other asset. However, only Flash MX can export the content in a SWF file, and it will only play in a browser with Flash 6 or later plug-in. With this feature, you can export it as a QuickTime movie instead. You could export *any* Flash movie in the QuickTime format, but SWF Flash is much more efficient for Flash content.

Projectors

The *Windows Projector* and *Macintosh Projector* formats will export self-playing Flash movies that don't require the Flash plug-in. The catch is that these formats are much larger in file size and won't play in a Web browser. This format is an ideal way to distribute your work on a disk. You could create a multimedia portfolio with this option and save it on a CD-ROM disk.

As their names imply, the Windows Projector will only play on Windows computers and the Macintosh Projector will only play on Macintosh computers. Be sure you don't give the Macintosh Projector to someone who has a Windows computer or vice versa. On a CD-ROM, you should be able to save both versions to make everyone happy.

◎◎ Working with the Published Files

The Publish feature is the most convenient way to generate an HTML page that embeds a SWF file. When you click on the Publish button in the Publish Settings window, it will save files in the formats you have selected. If you've selected both the *Flash* and *HTML* formats, this will save a SWF file and an HTML file in the same folder as the original Flash work file.

If your site or Web page is just the Flash movie, you can copy these files as-is to a Web site. However, it's more likely that you would want to integrate the Flash movie with text and other images on the page, and sometimes other Flash movies. In these cases, you'll need to use tools outside of Flash.

Publishing Flash with Dreamweaver and GoLive

Macromedia Dreamweaver and Adobe GoLive are HTML programs that free you from having to edit HTML code by hand. Once you have a Flash SWF file, you can use either program to place it directly on a Web page. They will add the necessary embed code for the HTML page and offer panels for setting the standard parameters, much like Flash's Publish feature.

Either program recognizes the HTML created by Flash's Publish feature and allows you to alter it. You can open the HTML file created by Flash to select, copy, and reposition the Flash content. All of the existing embed parameters will be intact and fully editable there. (However, if you use JavaScript for plug-in detection, everything will copy over just fine, but it won't be as simple to edit.)

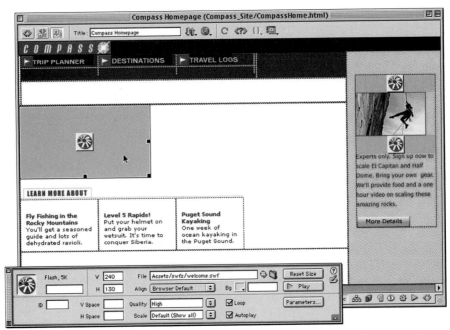

Figure 6.9 Dreamweaver (pictured here) and GoLive allow you to visually arrange Flash movies with other elements on an HTML page.

Editing HTML by Hand

If you don't have access to a program such as Dreamweaver or GoLive but you know some HTML, you can integrate the Flash HTML by hand. This section focuses only on the HTML that embeds a Flash SWF file, so you'll have to consult another book such as the *Web Wizard's Guide to HTML* to learn how to compose a complete HTML page.

First, open the HTML file saved by Flash (the one you saved using File→Publish Settings) with a text editing program (BBEdit, Macromedia HomeSite, or Microsoft Word). Copy everything from the opening `<OBJECT>` tag to the closing `</OBJECT>` tag from within that file (see Figure 6.10).

Next, open a second HTML file (the one that is composed for your actual Web site) in the same text editing program. Paste the copied code from the first HTML file where you want the Flash movie to appear.

Flash generates comment tags for all the text in a movie. Starting with `<!--URL's used in the movie -->`, these tags won't appear in a Web browser, but they do make the content of your Flash movie more accessible for searching. You can copy this over too.

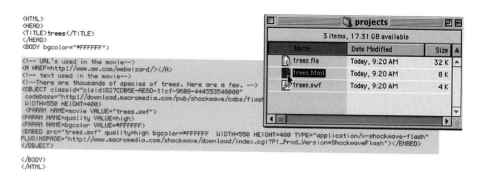

Figure 6.10 Opening the HTML file saved by the Publish feature; and selecting the embed code with a text-editing program.

☆**WARNING** **Changing the File Location**

Your Flash movie will never be seen if a Web page can't find it. The name of the SWF file (e.g., trees.swf) should be in two places in the HTML. If you move the SWF file to a location relative to the HTML file or rename it, be sure to change the HTML in both places to reflect this.

HTML from Scratch

Some HTML purists may want to embed Flash content entirely by hand. There are even a few parameters you can add this way that are not available from the Publish feature. After saving a SWF file, the following HTML is the bare minimum to embed it in a Web page:

```
<EMBED SRC="mymovie.swf" WIDTH="550" HEIGHT="400">
</EMBED>
```

This code only works for Web browsers with the proper plug-in installed. If the appropriate Flash plug-in is not installed, it will show up as a broken plug-in icon (see Figure 6.8). Also, it adds no parameters to control attributes such as the display quality. The above code is adequate only if you're quickly mocking up an HTML page. See the Online References section at the end of this chapter for more information about embedding Flash movies by hand.

◎◎ Testing in a Web Browser

Control→Test Movie is a good test for a Flash movie, but the most accurate test is in an actual Web browser. Browser testing is an important part of developing any Web content. The objective is to emulate the conditions in which your movie would be viewed in the real world. This will better ensure that your content will work as intended for your audience.

Testing Flash does not have to be as rigorous as testing complex, HTML-only pages. HTML can render (appear) differently on each brand and version of browser (e.g., Internet Explorer 5.5 for Windows vs. Netscape Navigator 4.7 for Macintosh).

Since all Flash content requires the same plug-in, it should play the same everywhere. But there still are some differences, especially in rendering performance.

You should test the SWF file itself and the HTML that embeds it. If your movie is confined to animation and basic actions, a test on your everyday browser should be adequate. However, if you start to use ActionScript intensively in your work, thorough testing will be essential. The biggest factor is the different versions of the Flash plug-in. If someone has a Flash 4 plug-in on a Macintosh, will they experience the same thing as someone using a Flash 6 plug-in on Windows? The surest way to know is to try it out.

☆ **SHORTCUT Use Your Friends**

You don't need to own a bank of computers to test a page thoroughly. Visit a friend who's got low-end equipment or go to a computer lab where you know there's an older model computer. Do the same if you need to borrow a Windows or Macintosh computer. If you've got access to a Web server, place your files there temporarily where no one would find them inadvertently. Then e-mail the address to friends and ask them to test your movie. Be sure to tell them what to look for (e.g., Does the movie halt unnaturally anywhere?").

Depending on whether you're using Windows or Macintosh, find a computer with the other platform and test it there too. Try different versions of the plug-in, too. (In the Online References section at the end of this chapter, there is a link to download old Flash plug-ins for testing.)

In each case, load the movie and look at how it displays. Try out all of the buttons and actions, and play all of the sounds. See the checklist under the "Testing Movies" section earlier in this chapter. Try your best to "break it"—to cause an error. You would rather it fail now when you can fix it quietly than have it fail for everyone once it's on the Web. Once your movie is live on a Web site, you should test it again.

◎◎ Accommodating Older Plug-ins

Since most of today's Web browsers include the Flash plug-in, it is rare that someone in your audience would not have it. A more common situation may occur if you create a Flash SWF file with newer features. Even if someone has the Flash plug-in, it may not be the latest version.

Which Version Is Appropriate for Your Audience?

First, you may want to consider how important those latest features are to your project. In many cases, where you aren't relying on much ActionScript, you can confine your project to Flash 4 features. Then everyone with a Flash 4 plug-in or later will be able to see your Flash work in all its glory. If you can orient your movie to Flash 3, that's all the better.

For an experimental art site or a cutting-edge entertainment site, then go head-first into all of the latest Flash features. If someone doesn't have the correct plug-in in this case, they'd be more motivated to take the time to install the new one.

If the Flash movie is an ad banner or for an e-commerce site or anything for a mass audience, it's more critical that it work seamlessly for everyone. In this case, you should produce something compatible with the Flash 3 plug-in.

Creating SWF Files for Older Players

The Publish feature can help you save Flash movies that are compatible with older versions of the Web browser player (plug-in). There are only a few things you need to do.

☆ First, go to the Flash window from File→Publish Settings and set the Version parameter to the older version number (e.g., Flash 4).

☆ Once you have set the Version to something lower in the Publish settings, Flash will warn you in the Actions window (or when you use Control→Test Movie) if you add an action that is not compatible with that lower version. You'll have to rewrite or remove any offending actions. For example, any dot syntax statements (covered in Chapter Seven) may have to be rewritten with *Tell Target* statements and slash syntax (covered in Chapter Four).

☆ If you want to use MP3 sound compression, only Flash 4 and later versions support it. You'll need to change it to ADPCM for Flash 3 or earlier compatibility.

☆ Players earlier than Flash 6 do not support embedded video created in Flash MX.

A Choice of Strategies

If you are creating a Flash SWF file to support older plug-ins, you could serve this file to everyone who has at least that version of Flash. If it's optimized for Flash 4, those with Flash 5 and Flash 6 plug-ins will see the same content. Use the HTML template described earlier to detect for the Flash 4 (or greater) plug-in and serve a GIF image to anyone else.

A second strategy would be to serve a version of the Flash SWF file that's only compatible with a newer plug-in. To those who don't have the appropriate plug-in, you would display a short message with a link to Macromedia's Web site to download the latest version. Flash doesn't include an HTML template for this, but look for it on the Web site for this book.

The ideal strategy would be to serve one version with all the latest features to those who have the appropriate plug-in installed and another for everyone else. This takes more work, however. For Flash 5 or Flash MX, don't hold back on using whatever ActionScript or sound compression you want. After you export a SWF file with those features, go back to your work file and replace or remove every feature that isn't supported by the lower version player (e.g., Flash 4 or Flash 3) and export a SWF file to support that version. Look for the Flash Deployment Kit in the Online References at the end of this chapter to help you generate the HTML for this method.

☆**TIP**   **Providing for Different Connection Speeds**

You can follow a similar strategy regarding file size. You could offer a richer version of the file that's much larger for users who have a fast connection speed, and a leaner version for everyone else. There's not an easy way to test for connection speed, so you'll have to offer your users a choice of HTML links to get to one of the two files: "Rich Version" vs. "Fast Version."

Accommodating Older Plug-ins

◎◎ Bringing It to the Web

When your Flash movie is ready for the world, it's time to transfer it to a Web server. If you already use an **FTP** program, you can transfer Flash SWF files with that. Be sure you copy the SWF files, the HTML files, and any other image files you may have saved with the Publish feature. Post everything except for the work files that you used in the Flash program (e.g., filename.fla).

If you are unsure of how to use FTP, look for links in the Online References section of this chapter. Also, ask your server administrator or Internet service provider for help.

Once you have transferred the files, test them again in a Web browser to be sure nothing is amiss. Consult the earlier section on testing in a Web browser.

☆**WARNING MIME Settings**

You must be sure that your Web server's MIME settings are set up for SWF Flash files. This will ensure that Flash movies will play on all browsers. Whoever manages your Web server should be able to do this for you. There's a link in the Online References section of this chapter for more information.

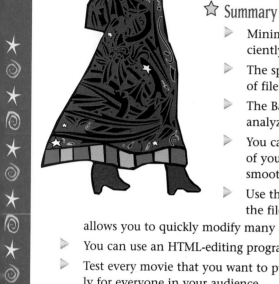

☆ Summary

⯈ Minimize the file size of a Flash movie by building it efficiently and maximizing compression.

⯈ The speed of the display of a Flash movie is independent of file size, but also important.

⯈ The Bandwidth Profiler helps you test your movie and analyze how well it downloads or streams.

⯈ You can create a loading sequence to ensure that enough of your movie will load at the start to play through smoothly.

⯈ Use the Publish feature (Edit→Publish Settings) to generate the files you need to publish your project. This feature allows you to quickly modify many attributes of the HTML and Flash files.

⯈ You can use an HTML-editing program to adapt the Flash HTML to your purposes.

⯈ Test every movie that you want to publish in a Web browser. Make sure it works correctly for everyone in your audience.

☆ Online References

Bad Bandwidth, Good Design
`http://www.webmonkey.com/98/42/index0a.html`

General Information for Exporting Flash Movies
`http://www.macromedia.com/support/flash/publishexport`

Adobe Go Live
`http://www.adobe.com/products/golive`

Macromedia Dreamweaver
`http://www.macromedia.com/software/dreamweaver`

Coding by Hand: How to Write Flash HTML by Hand
`http://www.macromedia.com/support/flash/ts/documents/tn4150.html`

All about Flash Plug-in Detection and the Flash Deployment Kit
`http://www.macromedia.com/support/flash/detection.html`

Plug-in Detection Kit
`http://www.moock.org/webdesign/flash/detection/moockfpi`

Download Old Flash Players for Testing
`http://www.macromedia.com/support/flash/ts/documents/oldplayers.htm`

Browser Support
`http://www.macromedia.com/support/flash/ts/documents/`
`browser_support_matrix.htm`

Netscape Browser Archives
`http://www.netscape.com/download/archive`

Using Cute FTP for Windows
`http://www.webmonkey.com/98/42/index2a.html`

Using Macintosh Fetch for FTP
`http://www.webmonkey.com/98/41/index4a.html`

How to Use FTP
`http://www.ftpplanet.com/ftpresources/basics.htm`

Server MIME Settings for Flash
`http://www.FlashCentral.com/Tech/Server`

☆ Review Questions

1. What is a synonym for file size when referring to content transmitted over the Internet? How does it relate to Flash?

2. Describe two strategies that help reduce the file size of a Flash movie.

3. What feature in Flash allows someone to view the first part of a movie while the rest of it downloads?

4. List three features in a Flash movie that can contribute to rendering problems.

5. Which feature do you use to search for a specific word displayed in a Flash work file?

6. How would you simulate how the movie would play when downloaded over a 28.8K modem? Explain how the Bandwidth Profiler shows where a movie would pause because of download bottlenecks.

7. Which tab in the Publish feature (Edit→Publish Settings) displays the default sound compression for a movie?

8. Which tab in the Publish feature reveals the option to scale a Flash movie on a Web page?

9. What is the surest way to test a Flash file?

10. How would you accommodate people in your audience who have version 3 of the Flash plug-in?

☆ Hands-On Exercises

1. With any Flash file from a previous exercise, export two SWF files of the same project. One version should be as large as possible. The other should be as small as possible.

2. Go to the Web Wizard Web site (http://www.aw.com/webwizard) and download the link *Chapter Six Exercises*. Open the file called *profile.fla*. From the

Bandwidth Profiler use the Show Streaming feature (28.8 connection speed) and test how it plays. Remove the bitmap image in the second keyframe and test it again. Change the compression of the sound called *background track* to MP3 with a bit rate of 8kbps and test it again. Listen to the sound and watch how the movie streams. Change the sound compression to what you think works best. Explain your choice.

3. Open the exercise file named *optimize.fla*. Analyze the movie with the Bandwidth Profiler and remove the bottlenecks. Explain what you did and why.

4. Create a "loading" sequence that will play until the entire movie has been loaded. Get extra credit if you can make it effective without using the word "loading."

5. Use the Publish feature to save the same movie as a Flash 5 SWF file. Select an HTML template to supply a GIF image to browsers that do not have the Flash 5 plug-in installed. Publish another SWF file for the Flash 3 plug-in and embed that in a separate HTML page.

CHAPTER SEVEN

EASING INTO ACTIONSCRIPT

I n Chapter Four, you learned how to apply basic actions. They have been a part of Flash since the earliest versions and are an easy way to add interactivity to any Flash movie. This chapter picks up where Chapter Four left off, explaining how to write some of the same actions by hand and introducing others. Once this footing is established, you'll learn how to construct dot syntax statements and apply other scripting ingredients, opening the door to the full power of interactivity in Flash. This chapter will get you started writing simple ActionScripts that create movie clips and manipulate them. From this foundation you could continue to learn more advanced ActionScript to eventually create robust games and Web-based applications.

◎◉ Chapter Objectives

☆ Show how to write basic actions by hand
☆ Demonstrate how to apply built-in functions
☆ Read and manipulate the properties of movie clips
☆ Understand object-oriented scripting and how to apply dot syntax

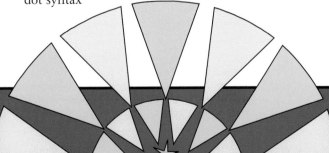

☆ Explore the flexibility of ActionScript by applying conditionals, operators, and variables

☆ Show how to create a custom function

☆ Discuss strategies for creating better ActionScript and fixing bugs

◎◎ Designing with ActionScript

All of the material covered in Chapter Four, from the *Stop* action to *Tell Target*, is a form of ActionScript. In the Actions panel, what you saw in the text pane is ActionScript code. By learning to write ActionScript directly, you will be able to adapt these predefined actions the way you want or build your own.

☆ **WARNING** **Pre-Flash 5 ActionScript**

This chapter is oriented to ActionScript created in Flash 5 and later. Some of what you learn here will not be compatible with older versions of the Flash player (or Web browser plug-in). In the Flash window from File→Publish Settings, change the Version option to Flash 4 or Flash 3 (depending on which version of the Flash player you want to support). Once you do this, Flash will warn you if you write ActionScript that is not compatible with that earlier player.

ActionScript gives designers access to creating behaviors with Flash that previously were the domain of hard core programmers who were trained in languages such as Java and C++. At first, you may find ActionScript challenging to learn, but it is much easier than those languages. Plus, the Flash program has built-in features to help you.

An **object-oriented language**, ActionScript refers to everything as **objects**: text, sounds, symbol instances, even the movie itself. These objects have their own names and hierarchies which identify them. This is the path that you used for *tellTarget()* in Chapter Four. Each object also has specific **properties** and **methods** that give it characteristics and behaviors. The color property of a ball may be red, and a movie clip's method can make it play.

◎◎ From Basic Actions to ActionScript

You can set the Actions panel to either Normal mode or Expert mode. When the Actions panel is set to Normal mode, you make selections from its menus and Flash writes the ActionScript for you in that pane. This is what you were doing in Chapter Four.

In Figure 7.1, you can see what happens in Normal mode when you click on the event handler `on(release)`. This reveals several **parameter** choices with checkboxes. When you select other actions, corresponding parameter choices accompany them. These options present specific choices, ensuring that you write error-free actions. The options are predetermined, which limits how you can compose ActionScript.

The Expert mode allows you to type freely within the text pane. This allows you infinite control over authoring actions, but you are also responsible for writing correct ActionScript code. In this chapter, you will be working directly with the text pane. To create a *Stop* action, you would type:

```
stop();
```

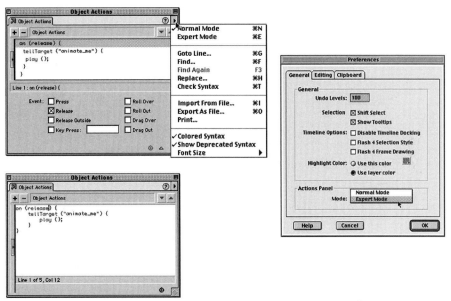

Figure 7.1 Changing the Actions panel from Normal mode (top) to Expert mode (bottom).

Like a kid removing the training wheels from a bicycle, it's time to set the Actions panel to Expert mode. To change this mode for a single action, choose *Expert Mode* from the panel options in the upper-right corner of the Action panel (see Figure 7.1). If you want to set this mode as the default for all actions, change this setting in Edit→Preferences. When needed, you can always change it back to Normal mode later.

While working with ActionScript, you can switch back and forth between Normal mode and Expert mode. When you want the guidance of the parameter menus, use Normal mode; and for the ease of direct editing, use the Expert mode. When you switch from Expert mode to Normal mode, Flash will also check your script and warn you if there is an error.

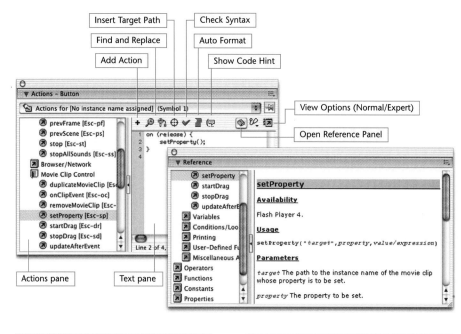

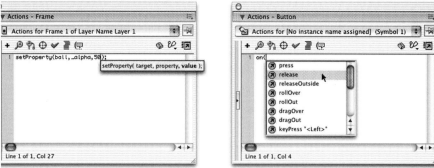

Figure 7.2 The Flash MX Actions panel and Reference panel (top). A code hint is visible (bottom left). Code hint with pop-up menu (bottom right).

◎◎ Revisiting tellTarget()

Chapter Four introduced the *tellTarget()* action. Before Flash 5 ActionScript, *tellTarget()* was required to apply an action from one object (a button or frame) to another object (a movie clip). This is what displayed in the text pane when the action was added to the button:

☆ **FLASH MX**   **A Revised Actions Panel**

The Flash MX Actions panel is slightly rearranged. You can write the same ActionScript in the Flash MX Actions panel as you would in Flash 5, but the newer panel adds a few features to assist you. Figure 7.2 points out several of these features.

The new Reference panel is an interactive reference that outlines how to use a selected action. Right-click on an action in the actions pane or text pane and choose the *View Reference* option to open the Reference panel with the summary of that action. You can also click on the Reference icon on the Actions panel to do the same thing.

You don't have to remember exactly how to format an action in Expert mode. As you use ActionScript, code hints will pop up in a menu to help you write correct code. If the code hint goes away, you can click on the *Show Code Hint* button to reveal it again.

The Check Syntax (also available in Flash 5) and Auto Format features check your code and help you format it more neatly. There is also a new find feature and a few other niceties that you will discover as you use this panel.

In Flash MX there is no setting for Normal or Expert mode from Edit→Preferences. Whichever mode you choose from the Actions panel will persist for every action until you change it again.

```
on(release) {
    tellTarget("Apple/Seed") {
        play();
    }
}
```

☆ **TIP**   **ActionScript Notation**

Chapter Four refers to actions by conventional titles (e.g., *Play, Stop, Tell Target*). This chapter refers to actions in their ActionScript format. In this chapter you will instead see *play()*, *stop()*, and *tellTarget()*, written as they would appear in an actual ActionScript.

This chapter assumes you have an understanding of paths as explained in Chapter Four. To review, the essence of a *tellTarget()* action is its path. The section "Defining a Path" near the end of Chapter Four goes into detail on this. Looking at Figure 4.9, you could call an action from the Timeline of the *Tree* object to the *Seed* object in the *Apple* with the following absolute path: `_level0/Tree/Apple/Seed`. A relative path would be `Apple/Seed`.

To rewrite the Chapter Four action by hand, you need to know some **syntax**, which is like grammar. Syntax is the rules for formatting code. The *tellTarget()* action requires parentheses and quotation marks to contain the path to the target. A pair of braces also must follow that. Insert an action between the braces and you complete the ActionScript. The example below would target a *play()* action to the *Seed* movie clip.

```
tellTarget ("Apple/Seed") {
    play();
}
```

To assign this action to a button, you'll need to add an **event handler**. This determines when the mouse will trigger the action. When the mouse releases over the button (after it clicks down), an action contained by an event handler will execute. To apply an event handler, nest the *tellTarget()* action between opening and closing braces:

```
on(release) {
    tellTarget("Apple/Seed") {
        play();
    }
}
```

- event handler and open brace nest the `tellTarget()` action
- `tellTarget()` and its open brace nest the `play()` action
- `play()` action
- closing brace of `tellTarget()`
- closing brace of the `on(release)` event handler

This is the same *tellTarget()* action from Chapter Four, written directly in ActionScript. Following are examples of how to write a few essential actions.

◎◎ Applying Built-in Functions

The basic actions you applied in Chapter Four are built-in functions. Like any scripting language, you can apply built-in functions or create your own with ActionScript. Apply them to objects, such as the main movie or a movie clip instance, to manipulate them in a specific way. When a function is called, an object may disappear or a movie may play. Here's how to apply a few functions with ActionScript.

☆ **TIP**   **Use a Reference Guide**

A more complete explanation of ActionScript functions and other expressions is available from the ActionScript Dictionary under Flash's Help menu. You'll do even better with a comprehensive book such as *ActionScript: The Definitive Guide*.

These guides are essential to learning about other objects, properties, and methods. If you're content with functions like *stop()* and *play()*, you don't need the reference, but if you want to know how to use *Math.random* or *attachMovie()*, you'll find it indispensable.

---

gotoAndPlay()

From Chapter Four, you should be familiar with the *gotoAndPlay()* function. Apply this function to a button and a mouse click can force the movie to jump to a specific frame. Here is how you would assign this action to a button.

```
on(release) {
    gotoAndPlay("start_animation");
}
```

The *gotoAndPlay()* function requires a parameter to indicate which frame to move to. To assign a parameter to a function, place it between the parentheses immediately following the function name. In the above example, `"start_animation"` tells the function that you want to move the playhead of the movie to a frame labeled *start_animation*.

The quotation marks are used in this case because *start_animation* is a literal name, not a number or a variable. Numerical data does not need the quotation marks, so you would direct the playhead to the 20th frame like this:

```
on(release) {
    gotoAndPlay(20);
}
```

☆**WARNING** **ActionScript Is Case Sensitive**

Whenever you write ActionScript, pay close attention to how words are capitalized. The action *gotoAndPlay()* is not necessarily the same thing as *GoToandplay()*.

setProperty()

Movie clips have several built-in properties including alpha value (transparency), position, and width. From Chapter Three, you should know how to change a few of these from the Effect or Transform panels (the Properties Inspector for Flash MX). Using ActionScript, you can change these properties, plus others, with the *setProperty()* function.

If a function requires more than one parameter, you must list them in a predetermined order. Placed between the single set of parentheses, they are separated by commas. The *setProperty()* function requires three parameters, in the following order:

1. The first parameter is the path to the target object. It takes the place of the *tellTarget()* path (e.g., *Tree*, *Tree/Apple*, */Orange*).

2. The second parameter defines the property to be set for that object (e.g., *_alpha*, *_xscale*, *_y*). You can identify a property because it usually begins with an underscore. Many of them are listed in the Properties submenu on the Actions panel.

3. The third parameter is the new numerical value set for the property (e.g., *100*, *20*, *0*).

Of course, you can set the alpha value of a symbol instance when building a Flash movie. But this ActionScript function allows it to be changed interactively, while the movie plays. If you add the following code to a button, your users can make the *Apple* object fade back:

```
on (rollOver) {
    setProperty("Tree/Apple", _alpha, 20);
}
```

The target `Tree/Apple` refers to a movie clip instance and `20` will be the new alpha value.

The Properties submenu on the Actions panel lists several properties for movie clips, and they are described in the ActionScript Dictionary (under the Help menu or from the Reference panel in Flash MX). You can apply the *setProperty()* function more than once to multiple properties. The script below will resize both the target clip's _xscale (percentage width) and _yscale (percentage height) to 200% (twice) its original size.

```
on (release) {
   setProperty("Tree/Apple", _xscale, 200);
   setProperty("Tree/Apple", _yscale, 200);
}
```

Figure 7.3 demonstrates how transformations are applied with *setProperty()*:

A: The original movie with a movie clip. The apple is nested within the tree movie clip.

B: The *setProperty()* function sets the apple's *_alpha* to *50*.

C: The *_xscale* and *_yscale* of the tree is set to *75*. Notice that its child (the apple) is scaled with it.

D: Only the *_xscale* property is set to *150*, and only to the apple.

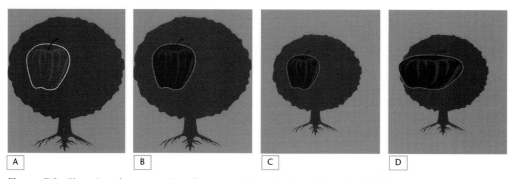

Figure 7.3 Changing the properties of a movie clip object and its nested child.

☆**TIP**   **Semicolons or Braces**

Either a semicolon or a brace follows every line of ActionScript code. A function such as `play();` or a statement such as `myVar=100;` requires a semicolon. An event handler, conditional, or anything else that contains other statements does not use a semicolon. Instead, it uses braces to contain other statements. Here is an event handler that contains a simple function:

```
on (release) {
   play();
}
```

---

trace()

The *trace()* function does not have an impact on how a movie plays, but it is used for debugging to check your work. This action has a single parameter. When you test a movie with Control→Test Movie, the value of that parameter will display in the Output window.

Anything in quotation marks will output exactly as you type it. Set up this ActionScript in the first frame of a movie:

```
trace("Here is my trace action.");
```

Use the Control→Text Movie command and the Output window will display, `Here is my trace action.` (You don't have to remember where this window is because it will pop up automatically.)

The *trace()* function will interpret a parameter without quotations. Later in this chapter, you will use it to display the value of a variable or a property in the Output window.

Although the *trace()* function is invisible in a published movie, using it more than a few times can degrade its performance. When you are ready to publish a final movie, go to File→Publish Settings and check *Omit Trace actions* in the Flash window. This will exclude all *trace()* actions from the published SWF file.

getProperty()

The *getProperty()* function works similarly to *setProperty()*, but is used to retrieve the current value of an object's property rather than change it. Since you aren't setting the value, you only need to supply two parameters: the object path and the property name. Use this function to find out the position, scale, or alpha value of a movie clip. This works for every movie clip property you can assign with *setProperty()*, plus a few others.

The _x and _y properties can be accessed by both the *getProperty()* and *setProperty()* functions. Like a mathematical graph, Flash ActionScript uses x and y coordinates to locate and position objects. The _x and _y properties refer to the x and y coordinates of the Flash Stage, measured in pixels. The _x property represents the position of an object starting from the left edge of the Stage. The _y property represents its position from the top downward.

The statement: `getProperty("Tree", _y);` will retrieve the numerical value of the _y property (position) of a movie clip named *Tree*.

Retrieving the value of a property means nothing unless you apply it somehow. The simplest way to apply it is with the *trace()* function. Later on, you'll learn how to use conditionals and variables to apply the *getProperty()* function in other ways.

Create a new Flash movie and place an instance of a movie clip on the Stage. Name it *myclip* and then add the following ActionScript to the main Timeline of the movie:

```
trace("This is the _x value:");
trace(getProperty("myclip", _x));
trace("This is the _y value:");
trace(getProperty("myclip", _y));
```

Test the movie, and read the Output window. It should display the following:

```
This is the _x value:
178
This is the _y value:
185
```

Leave the Output window open as you return to the movie. Reposition the movie clip on the Stage and test the movie again. The second test should output different numerical values because you moved the movie clip, changing its position (_x and _y properties).

There are several properties that are read-only, meaning that they cannot be changed with *setProperty()*. One is *_currentframe*, which checks the location of the playhead in a movie or movie clip. Remember the soundtrack movie clip in Chapter Five? You can use *_currentframe* to see where it is set to see if the soundtrack is playing or not. Open that movie and add this action to a new button on the main Timeline. The following assumes you have named the target movie clip *soundtrack*:

```
on(release) {
    trace(getProperty("soundtrack", _currentframe));
}
```

When you test the movie, first click the new button with the *trace()* action and check the Output window. Next, click the *Play* button that starts the sound track. Then click the button with the *trace()* action again, and check the Output window one more time. There should be a different value.

☆ **TIP**   **Building a Better Loading Message**

The *_framesloaded* property checks how much of a file has been downloaded. Since the *ifFrameLoaded()* action from Chapter Four is being deprecated, you can create the same functionality with this property and an *if* statement (covered later in this chapter). You could expand upon it to create a more accurate loading message that reflects how much has downloaded.

duplicateMovieClip()

Use the *duplicateMovieClip()* function to create new instances of a movie clip symbol. This function will duplicate any instance that is already placed on the Stage. Supply the following parameters:

1. The target movie clip instance that you want to duplicate

2. The name of the new instance you are creating

3. The depth value of the new clip

```
duplicateMovieClip("Tree", "Tree2", 2);
```

This function will duplicate the clip named *Tree* as a new clip named *Tree2* with a depth value of *2*. This will add a second instance to the Stage.

The depth value determines how duplicated clips are layered, similar to the level parameter for *loadMovie()*. A movie clip with a higher depth value will appear in front of those with lower values. When you generate more than one clip with same depth value, the second duplicate will replace the first. To create more than one duplicate, increment the depth value each time.

This will replace the tree duplicated in the last example with a pear:

```
duplicateMovieClip("Pear", "Pear2", 2);
```

This will leave the tree alone, duplicating a pear to layer 3:

```
duplicateMovieClip("Pear", "Pear2", 3);
```

By itself, *duplicateMovieClip()* is fairly useless since it places an instance of a movie clip directly on top of the original instance with no visible difference. Combine the *duplicateMovieClip()* function with the *SetProperty()* function and you can create instances of the same movie clip in different positions, or with other properties changed.

```
on (release) {
    duplicateMovieClip("Tree","Tree2",2);
    setProperty("Tree",_x,100);
    setProperty("Tree",_y,50);
}
```

This action will create a copy of the *Tree* object named *Tree2* and place it 100 pixels to the right and 50 pixels down from the upper-left corner of the Stage. A negative value for the third parameter would move the target object upward or to the left, off the Stage. You can apply this to a nested movie clip like this:

```
on (release) {
    duplicateMovieClip("Tree/Apple","Apple2",2);
    setProperty("Tree/Apple2",_x,0);
    setProperty("Tree/Apple2",_y,0);
}
```

A nested clip is positioned within its parent object. Rather than aligning the *Apple* clip to the upper-left corner of the Stage, this script will align it to the **registration point** of the *Tree* clip.

☆ **SHORTCUT Where a Movie Clip Aligns**

Every symbol has a registration point, displayed as a set of small crosshairs (see Figure 7.4). This is what ActionScript uses to align and position objects. The _x and _y properties of a movie clip correspond to the registration point of the original symbol. You can reposition the artwork of a symbol relative to its registration point when you edit it.

While editing the symbol, select all of the artwork and move it to the desired position on the Stage relative to the registration point. If it is a multiple-frame symbol, you'll have to use the *Edit Multiple Frames* option. Use the Align panel with the Stage button depressed to align one edge or the center of the selected artwork to the registration point. Alternately, you can use the Info panel to position objects.

As you apply the *duplicateMovieClip()* function and combine it with *setProperty()*, you can create artwork and transform it completely with ActionScript. Use *duplicateMovieClip()* several times to create multiple instances of symbol in different places. Apply *setProperty()* repeatedly to create animation without adding a single keyframe to the movie.

☆ **FLASH MX**   The *createEmptyMovieClip()* **Function**

In Flash 5, you are able to do some great things with the *duplicateMovieClip()* function. However, it depends on your manually placing a movie clip on the Stage when you author the movie. Flash MX introduces the *createEmptyMovieClip()* method. Along with several new drawing methods, you can create scripts to generate artwork completely from scratch. This is a powerful addition to ActionScript. Imagine a Flash movie that allows members of your audience to draw their own artwork, or watch a movie that generates original art by itself.

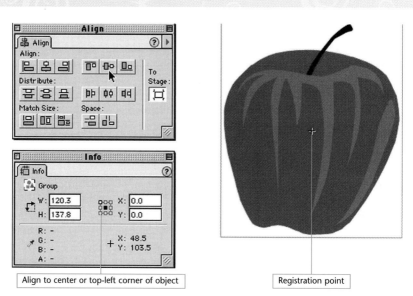

Align to center or top-left corner of object | Registration point

Figure 7.4 Use the Align or Info panel to reposition the artwork in a symbol relative to its registration point.

Writing Scripts in Dot Syntax

From the *tellTarget()* lesson in Chapter Four, you should have a head start on understanding **dot syntax**. Dot syntax utilizes the path targets you are familiar with from the *tellTarget()* action, except with dots instead of slashes. That's only the most obvious distinction. Starting with Flash 5, ActionScript became an object-oriented programming language. Dot syntax is a key ingredient, allowing you to access the full power of ActionScript. Although Flash still supports *tellTarget()* and its slash syntax, dot syntax is the future of ActionScript.

Dot Syntax vs. Slash Syntax Notation

Up to this point, this chapter has been using slash syntax to assign paths. You can use dot syntax notation in place of slash syntax for any of the previous examples. Dot syntax is an alternative to the slash syntax notation you used in Chapter Four, but it is only recognized by Flash 5 and later versions. The dot syntax path `Apple.Tree` gets you to the same place as `Apple/Tree`.

If you want to target something at a level up the hierarchy or to write an absolute path, there are a couple of keywords to learn. Chapter Three discussed how to nest symbols. A symbol which contains another symbol is a *parent* to that symbol. These keywords are formally used in relative paths.

☆ Looking at Figure 4.8, from the Timeline of *Apple*, the path `_parent` would target the Timeline of the *Tree* instance.

☆ From the *Tree* movie clip, the path `_parent.Orange` targets the Timeline of the *Orange* symbol. It's the same path as `../Tree` in slash syntax.

For an absolute path, the object `_level0` works the same in either slash syntax or dot syntax. However, the keyword `_root` replaces the initial slash in dot syntax to target the main Timeline of the current movie.

☆ The path `_root.Tree` would target the *Tree* instance from anywhere within the example in Figure 4.8. In slash syntax, it would be `/Tree`.

☆ The path to the main Timeline would simply be `_root`.

Appending a Method or Property to the Path

Dot syntax not only references an object's path, but also its properties and methods. A method does essentially the same thing as a function except that it belongs to an object. Several functions double as methods. One example is *play()*. It does the same thing either as a function or as a method, but as a method it belongs to a movie clip.

To invoke it as a method, append it to an object's path. With dot syntax, you can write a *play()* method like this:

```
on(release) {
    Apple.Seed.play();
}        └─path─┘  └─method─┘
```

You've seen how dot syntax replaces *tellTarget()* when assigning a path. It also supplants the *getProperty()* and *setProperty()* functions. With dot syntax, you can access an object's properties directly. As you would do with a method, append a property to an object's path.

Earlier, the getProperty function was used like this:

```
getProperty("Tree/Apple",_y);
```

With dot syntax, you can rewrite the function like this:

```
getProperty("Tree.Apple",_y);
```

or access the property directly like this:

```
Tree.Apple._y;
```

If you become more advanced with ActionScript, you can use dot syntax to create new properties and methods for objects. For this chapter, we'll keep it to built-in properties and methods.

When an Object Targets Itself

If an object applies a method or property to itself, you do not need a path. The relative path to the current Timeline is implied. For example, an action on the Timeline of a movie clip to stop itself would be simply:

```
stop();
```

For clarity, an object can target itself with the keyword *this*:

```
this.stop();
```

You can start the relative path to another object with the *this* keyword. From the Timeline of the *Tree* in the previous example, you could stop the *Apple* clip like so:

```
this.Apple.stop();
```

☆ **SHORTCUT** **Trace the Absolute Path of Any Movie Clip**

Using *this* as the parameter, apply the *trace()* function to an object to display its absolute path. Open a new movie and type `trace(this);` as an action in the first keyframe of the main Timeline. The Output window should display `_level0`, the path to the current object, the main Timeline.

Add a trace function to the Timeline of the *Apple* movie clip used in previous examples:

```
trace("This is the path to the Apple: ");
trace(this);
```

It should display the absolute path to that clip: `_level0.Tree.Apple`.

A Dot Syntax Tale

Another way to look at object-oriented programming and dot syntax is as if it were a sentence. The path is a noun and the method is a verb relating to the noun. To be more accurate, the path is an objective noun, like in the sentence, "Walk the dog." *Walk* is the method (or action) and *dog* is the object. Here is how this would be written in dot syntax:

```
dog.walk();
```

Let's say you're not with the dog. You're on the street asking a favor of your neighbor who happens to be more fluent in object-oriented languages than in English. Right now, your dog is in the kitchen inside your house. The neighbor asks in broken English what you want her to do. You reply in dot syntax:

`myHouse.kitchen.dog.walk();` (see Figure 7.5)

Objects also have properties such as color, size, and position. ActionScript considers these to be objects too, and they can be read and manipulated. Your neighbor wants to know the color of the dog. In English, you could say, "The color of the dog inside the kitchen in my house is brown." In dot syntax, you would say:

`myhouse.kitchen.dog._color == brown;`

Figure 7.5 Everyday conversation in object-oriented dot syntax.

☆**WARNING   No Dot Syntax for Older Flash Players**

Dot syntax is the way of the future for ActionScript. However, keep in mind that Flash players (i.e., Web browser plug-ins) previous to Flash 5 do not recognize dot syntax. If you want to be compatible with the Flash 3 or Flash 4 player, you'll need to stick with *tellTarget()* and use the slashes instead of dots to target an object. Flash 3 supports fewer actions, but for Flash 4, you can access an object's properties with the *getProperty()* and *setProperty()* functions.

Applying Dot Syntax to Methods and Properties

If you invoke the *setProperty()* function for several objects and properties, your script can become quite lengthy. You can save yourself a lot of typing by using dot syntax instead. With dot syntax, you could rewrite the earlier *duplicateMovieClip()* example like this:

```
on (release) {
    duplicateMovieClip("Tree/Apple", "Apple2", 2);
    Tree.Apple2._x = 0;
    Tree.Apple2._y = 0;
}
```

The equals sign assigns the value on its right to the object's property on its left. In this case the value 0 is assigned to the _x and _y properties of *Apple2*.

Similarly, the function *duplicateMovieClip()* can be invoked as a method. Omit the path parameter between the parentheses and assign it with dot syntax.

```
on (release) {
    Tree.Apple.duplicateMovieClip("Apple2",2);
    Tree.Apple2._x = 100;
    Tree.Apple2._y = 50;
}
```

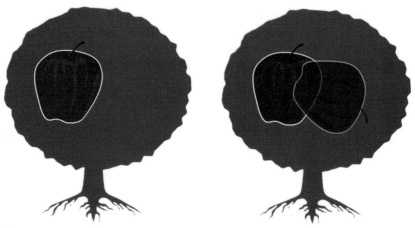

Figure 7.6 Duplicating a movie clip and changing multiple properties at once.

You'll really appreciate dot syntax when you want to set several properties at once. To get the effect in Figure 7.6, add the following ActionScript to a button:

```
on (release) {
    Tree.Apple1.duplicateMovieClip("Apple2", 2);
    Tree.Apple2._x = 200;
    Tree.Apple2._y = 150;
    Tree.Apple2._alpha = 60;
    Tree.Apple2._rotation = 105;
}
```

The with( ) Statement

If you want to change several properties or methods for a single object, you can shorten things even more. Why not get rid of the redundant `Tree.Apple2` path in the last example? You could use *tellTarget()* to assign the path to several statements at once, but that action is now deprecated in favor of dot syntax and the *with()* statement. It essentially does the same thing, but it's part of dot syntax. Apply a series of statements to one object by nesting them inside a *with()* statement.

```
on (release) {
    Tree.Apple1.duplicateMovieClip("Apple2", 2);
    with (Tree.Apple2) {
        _x = 200;
        _y = 150;
        _alpha = 60;
        _rotation = 105;
    }
}
```

◎◉ Setting Requirements with Conditionals

A conditional statement is a gatekeeper to a function. The most popular is the *if* statement. When a condition is met, the code contained by the *if* statement, a function or other script, is executed. If a condition is not met, that code is ignored.

The If Statement

Here is the syntax of a basic *if* statement:

Parameter between parentheses is criteria that must be met.

```
if (condition) {
    someFunction();
}
```

As you would for an event handler, you can insert any script between the braces.

The following script applies an *if* statement to the *getProperty()* function. This is based on the exercise in the pervious section that would check the frame position of the *soundtrack* movie clip. This assumes that the *soundtrack* clip was set up so that a keyframe at the 5th frame triggers the sound to play.

```
if (getProperty("soundtrack", _currentframe) == 5) {
    setProperty("Tree/Apple ", _alpha, 20);
}
```

The double equals sign, ==, is an **operator** that compares the *getProperty()* value to the numerical value. When this script is called, the *getProperty()* function will check to see if the *soundtrack* Timeline is at frame 5. If it is, *setProperty()* will change the alpha value of the *Apple* clip to 20, making it appear to fade out. If the soundtrack clip is at any other frame, nothing will happen.

But wait, we were just discussing dot syntax. This does the same thing, but more elegantly:

```
if (soundtrack._currentframe == 5) {
    Tree.Apple._alpha = 20;
}
```

The Else Statement

The optional *else* statement can be added to accommodate when a condition is not met. An *else* statement must follow an *if* statement, and it has no parameters. Like the *if* statement, a pair of braces follows it to contain some code. When the *if* condition is not met, the code contained within the *else* statement will be triggered. When the *if* condition is met, the *else* code will be ignored. You can place any valid ActionScript you want between the braces.

```
if (soundtrack._currentframe == 5) {
   Tree.Apple._alpha = 20;
}
else {
   Tree.Apple._alpha = 100;
}
```

If this script is called when the *soundtrack* clip is at frame 5, the alpha value of the *Apple* will be set to 20. If not, it will be set to 100.

The Else If Statement

Sometimes you want to set more than one condition. The *else if* statement allows you to add multiple conditions in case the first one is not met. It is constructed just like an *if* statement except it follows an *if* statement. Building on the soundtrack example, suppose you have more than one soundtrack clip on the Stage. The conditional could check each soundtrack clip to see its status.

```
if (soundtrack1._currentframe == 5) {
   Tree.Apple._alpha = 20;
}
else if (soundtrack2._currentframe == 5) {
   Tree.Apple._alpha = 50;
}
else if (soundtrack3._currentframe == 5) {
   Tree.Apple._alpha = 80;
}
else {
   Tree.Apple._alpha = 100;
}
```

This script will set the alpha value of *Apple* to different values depending on which of three soundtracks is playing. If none are playing, it will set it to 100.

> ☆ **TIP**   **Loop Statements**
>
> Loop statements are conditionals that allow you to repeat a portion of script many times under specified conditions. Consult your ActionScript reference for more on how to apply them.

◎◎ Using Variables and Operators

Variables are an invisible object in ActionScript. They are storage containers for numerical values, names, properties, and other types of information. Once information is stored in a variable, a script can later retrieve, change, or apply it.

Use variables as shorthand for information that is used more than once in a Flash movie. Once you store a name in a variable, you can retrieve it later as many times as you need it. As one example, you can get the property of an object and store its value in a variable. This would save you from having to look for a property of a movie clip every time you want to check its status.

Defining Variables

To define a variable, you must first create the storage container. **Declare** the variable. The best place to do this is in the first keyframe of the main Timeline of your movie, after any preloader (loading loop). Declare a variable with the word *var* followed by a space and the variable name. (Only use the word *var* the first time you invoke a specific variable.)

```
var first_name;
var last_name;
```

> ☆**WARNING** Rules for Variable Names
>
> You can use any letter of the alphabet and number for a variable name, but you must avoid using spaces or hyphens. For clarity, you can use an underscore character to separate two words (e.g., *first_name*). You must also start the variable name with a letter of the alphabet. The variable name *ball1* is allowed, but avoid *1ball*.
>
> Like functions, variable names are case sensitive, meaning you must capitalize or not capitalize a variable exactly the same whenever you store it or retrieve it. ActionScript will consider *first_name* and *First_Name* to be different variables.

Once you have declared a variable, you can **assign** a value to it. This stores information in the storage container. To do this, place an equals sign after a variable name, followed by the value you are assigning to it. If you are assigning words to a variable, enclose them with quotation marks. If you are assigning a numerical value, you can omit the quotation marks.

```
first_name = "Preston";
last_name = "Sturges";
age = 37;
```

You can also declare and assign a variable at the same time:

```
var first_name = "Preston";
var last_name = "Sturges";
var age = 37;
```

Retrieving Variables

Once a variable has been assigned, you can place its name within a function or other statement. When that ActionScript is triggered, Flash will look in the container for each variable name. The script will substitute each variable name with the value stored in its container. After declaring the variables above, use the following *trace()* function to retrieve and output their values:

```
trace (first_name);
trace (last_name);
trace (age);
```

When you test the movie, the Output window should display the following:

```
Preston
Sturges
37
```

Applying Operators to Variables and Properties

The previous section used the equals sign operator to assign a value to a variable. Operators are symbol characters that can combine expressions in various ways. Each one has predetermined roles for changing, specifying, or comparing the values of variables and properties. Some operators can perform basic mathematical functions such as adding and multiplying numbers.

Your ActionScript reference should have a complete list of operators, but here are a few essential ones.

Operator	Description
=	The equals sign, called the **assignment operator**, will assign a value to a variable or property. This was used earlier in this section. If a variable already exists, this will replace its value.

+	The plus sign adds to a number or text string. It will mathematically add numbers together or **concatenate** (join) text, property values, and variables. The examples below use variables, but will work the same with properties.
	
	`trace(20 + 1);` Will output the numerical value 21.
	
	`age = age + 1;` Changes the stored value of the variable.
	
	`trace(age + 1);` Adds 1 to the value of the variable age just for this trace() function. The stored value of the variable remains unchanged.
	
	`var first_name = "Preston";`
	`var last_name = "Sturges";`

Operator	Description
+ (*continued*)	`var full_name = first_name + " " + last_name;` Defines the variable full_name by combining (concatenating) the value of first_name, a space, and the value of last_name. `trace(full_name);` Will output `Preston Sturges`.
+=	These operators combine the previous two operators. This single operator will add to a variable *and* update its stored value. `var age = 20;` `age += 5;` Changes the value of the variable to 25 This is shorthand for: `age = age + 5;`
−, *, /	Use these operators to subtract, multiply, or divide numerical values. `trace(3 * 9);` Will output 27.
==	The double equals sign, also called the *equality operator*, is used to compare values. `if (soundtrack._currentframe == 5) { function(); }` Checks the value of the *_currentframe* property to see if it is 5.
!=	The opposite of the equality operator, the *inequality operator* compares values to see if they are *not* equivalent. `if (soundtrack._currentframe != 5) { function(); }` Checks the value of the *_currentframe* property to see if it is not 5.

<, >, <=, >=	The less than, greater than, less than or equal to, greater than or equal to operators compare values that aren't equal.
	
	`if (age < 21) {`
	`    trace ("Sorry, you cannot have a drink.");`
	`}` If the value of the variable age is a number less than 21, the *trace()* function will be called.

Combining Variables, Operators, and Properties

Combine all these ingredients and you are really putting ActionScript to work. And why not throw in a conditional for good measure? Here's how to apply everything you have learned up to this point.

First, open a new Flash movie and create a movie clip symbol of a red circle. Place an instance of that circle on the main Timeline, and name it *red_circle*.

Next, add the following script to the first keyframe of the movie.

```
stop();
var xyPosition = 0;
red_circle._x = xyPosition;
red_circle._y = xyPosition;
```

The *stop()* function will make sure that the movie does not play past the first frame. The second line declares the variable *xyPosition* and assigns an initial value of *0* to it. No matter where you place the *red_circle* clip on the Stage, the last two lines will initially place it at the upper-left corner of the Stage.

Next, place a button on the Stage and assign the following ActionScript to it. Once you have set this all up, test the movie and click the button several times (see Figure 7.7).

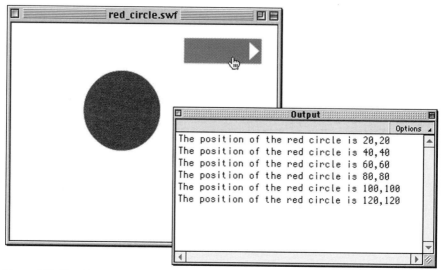

Figure 7.7 The Output window here displays the results of applying this ActionScript multiple times.

Each button click will trigger the following script.

```
on (release) {
if (red_circle._x < 300) {
    xyPosition += 20;
    } else {
        xyPosition = 0;
    }

    red_circle._x = xyPosition;
    red_circle._y = xyPosition;

    trace ("The position of the red circle is "
    + red_circle._x + "," + red_circle._y);
}
```

Checks if the position of red_circle is less than 300 pixels from the left edge of the Stage.

If condition is met, xyPosition is increased by 20.

If condition is not met, xyPosition is set to 0.

Moves red_circle to the new x and y positions.

Outputs the actual position of the circle.

Closes the on(release) event handler.

◎◎ Building a Custom Function

Like a variable, a custom function is a storage device. Rather than storing numbers and words, a function stores a working script. First you declare, or define, a function on the main Timeline of a movie and later you can call it from anywhere within the movie.

Declare a function that stores a *trace()* action:

```
function writeIt() {
    trace("Hello, my name is Riley.");
}
```

Once you have declared that function, you can call it by adding the following to a button:

```
on (release) {
    writeIt();
}
```

That's essentially it, but you can take things further. Define a parameter for the function, allowing the message to be changed each time the function is placed. Create a name for a parameter inside the function's parentheses (*myName* in the example below). Then repeat the parameter name somewhere within the function where, like a variable, it will be replaced when the function is called.

```
function writeIt(myName) {
    trace("Hello, my name is " + myName);
}
```

When you call the function, insert a name as the parameter, surrounded by quotation marks.

```
on (release) {
    writeIt("Riley");
}
```

When clicked, this example will output, `Hello, my name is Riley` in the output window. You can declare the following function to position the *red_circle* movie clip:

```
function moveCircle(xPosition,yPosition) {
    red_circle._x = xPosition;
    red_circle._y = yPosition;
}
```

Call the function, inserting the _x and _y values as the parameters to position the red circle.

```
on (release) {
    moveCircle(150,200);
}
```

◎◎ Writing Good Code

Throughout this chapter you have been exposed to rules that govern the structure of ActionScript. For example, a function must be followed by two parentheses, sometimes containing parameters:

```
gotoAndPlay(30);
```

Or, to assign literal words to a variable, you must enclose it in quotation marks:

```
var message1 = "Welcome to our Web site.";
```

These rules are essential to making your script work.

Even if you pay close attention to the rules, it is a rare ActionScript that works correctly on first try. Things slip by, and as you try new techniques, you'll inevitably have to go through some trial and error. Following are some strategies for writing clear code in the first place and that will help you fix what's broken.

Create an Action Layer

You can add frame actions to any keyframe in any layer of a Flash movie, but you'd be better off keeping them to a single layer. Create a dedicated layer in your movies just for actions, and name it *Actions*. This way you will be able to find them more quickly for editing and debugging.

Start Simple

Build complexity into your script incrementally. Start with a simple script that does one thing and test it out. When it's stable, add some complexity and test it again. Repeat this until the script is complete. Take these baby steps and you'll cut down on stress.

Use White Space

ActionScript generally ignores extra returns, indents, and spaces between elements. Use indents and returns to make your script more digestible, easier to read and edit. You'll make fewer errors if your script is formatted in a more readable way.

This is perfectly valid ActionScript:

```
on(release){red_ball._x+=20;red_ball._y+=20;}
```

But it's easier to read when formatted like this:

```
on (release) {
    red_ball._x += 20;
    red_ball._y += 20;
}
```

There are other places where a space can cause problems. Spaces are not allowed within names of variables, functions, or properties. They're also not allowed anywhere within an object's path. These statements will cause errors:

```
var full name = "Rafael Gonzales";
_level0 . Tree . Apple . _x = 50;
```

These are correct:

```
var full_name = "Rafael Gonzales";
_level0.Tree.Apple._x = 50;
```

You've got your ActionScript working well, but it's not formatted very neatly. Temporarily change the Actions window to Normal mode and then switch it back to Expert mode. Flash will neatly reformat your code for you.

Flash MX will format your scripts as you type. To reformat existing code, click the Auto Format button on the Actions panel (see Figure 7.2). To change where this feature adds spaces, choose *Auto Format Options* from the options menu of the Actions panel.

Comment Your Code

While you are first writing an ActionScript, you may have a pretty good idea of what is going on. If you, or someone else, comes back to it later, it may be difficult to decipher. Comment your code to explain what is there and how it works. Commenting doesn't make a script work any differently, but it is an important ingredient of good code.

Flash will ignore any line that begins with // marks, and you can surround several lines of comments with /* and */. Here are a few examples.

```
// This comment could describe the function below
function writeHead(headText) {
    trace("The headline is " + headText);
}

var mainHead = "The Best of Times"; // end of line comment
/*
#################################################
This is a longer comment that explains more in depth
what is going on in the script.
#################################################
*/
```

Also, use comment tags to hide lines of code. Through the process of elimination, you can isolate your errors this way. If you comment out a particular line of code and the script functions better, then you know to fix that line. Below, the *if* statement is disabled by comment tags.

```
// if (ball._x < 200) {
   ball._x += 6;
   ball._y += 4;
// }
```

Check Your Syntax

From the Actions panel, you can check your script as you work. Use the Check Syntax command from the panel's options menu. This will not catch every problem with a script, but it will alert you if you forgot a parameter or added an extra quotation mark.

Use your eyes as well. Proofread your code. Often a misspelled word or an errant punctuation mark can cripple an entire script.

Code Review

Four eyes are better than two. If you've been engrossed in your code for a while, it can impair your ability to spot even the most obvious errors. When you show your code to a friend, she will probably find that error right under your nose. This is also a good way for you both to learn from each other.

Test the Movie

When you use the Test Movie command, Flash first checks the syntax of the script and alerts you about any problems. If it detects any errors, the Output window will open and describe them. Pay attention to any messages displayed there.

While in this mode, choose Debug→List Objects to output a list of the path to every named object in the movie. Use Debug→List Variables to check the values of every variable at a particular point in the movie.

Once you have fixed the ActionScript errors that prevent the movie from playing, you should try it out in the preview window (Control→Test Movie). Test the script as it was intended (e.g., click a button) and how it wasn't intended (e.g., click and drag on different parts of the button). Is the behavior correct? You are trying to "break" the script or make it fail now so that it will be less likely to fail when you publish it on the Web. Ask your friends to try it out as well.

Use the trace() Function

Covered earlier in this chapter, use the *trace()* function liberally. Use it to check the value of a variable or property at any point in a script. If you use this function and it displays nothing in the Output window or something unexpected, that would be a clue to a bug in the script.

◎◎ What Else You Can Do with ActionScript

You should have learned enough in this chapter to begin creating some fairly sophisticated ActionScripts. However, this is only an introduction. With loads of sweat and imagination, you can go as far as you like. To learn more, check out the links at the end of this chapter or consult an ActionScript reference. Here are a few ActionScript features worth trying.

Movie Clip Events

Like button events, some events can be assigned to a movie clip so that it can trigger an ActionScript. A clip can instruct itself to move. The *enterFrame* event occurs every time a movie clip Timeline moves into any frame, causing an action to repeat indefinitely. Add this script to a movie clip and it will move itself diagonally across the Stage.

```
onClipEvent (enterFrame) {
    if (this._x < 400) {
        this._x += 6;
        this._y += 4;
    }
}
```

The *keyDown* event triggers an action when someone clicks any key on the keyboard. The *mouseMove* event tracks when the user moves the mouse anywhere within the Stage. You could translate the movement of the mouse to the behavior of the clip itself. This is a great way to add game-like interactivity. For a list of all the clip events, consult your ActionScript reference.

Smart Clips/Components

Smart clips are specialized movie clips with embedded variables and functions. They are pre-built modular scripts that require no tinkering with ActionScript. Some smart clips allow you to place interface widgets in your movie, such as checkboxes for forms or scroll bars to move through text. They also provide a means to adapt the same script for different Flash movies.

A few Smart Clips are included with the Flash program (In Flash 5, go to Window→Common Libraries→Smart Clips), and there are many posted online (see the Online References section). After adding a smart clip to your movie, customize it from the Clip Parameters panel.

> ☆ **FLASH MX**   **Goodbye Smart Clips, Hello Components**
>
> Components replace Smart Clips in Flash MX. The new Components panel is dedicated to them. Specify options from the Component Parameters panel.

Importing Variables, Text, and XML

If you are working with a writer who is editing the text for a project, it can be a bother if he has to ask you, as the Flash artist, to make each change in the Flash file. Or, if you are posting a daily news column, it would be quicker to type the text than to edit the Flash movie itself.

With Flash, you can create a SWF movie that will load variables and text from a simple text file, a file that someone can edit with any word processing program. You can even add a few basic HTML tags to the text to format it. Within the Flash movie, you could set up form fields that allow users to enter information that is sent to a CGI script on a Web server.

Flash is also built to work with XML, an interchangeable standard for marking up text and data and sharing it between different environments. Your movie can load data and interact with Web servers via XML, accessing the same content used by standard computer programs and Web pages. With XML support, Flash can be used for more robust Web applications such as a live chat application or an e-commerce site. There are a few online XML references listed at the end of this chapter.

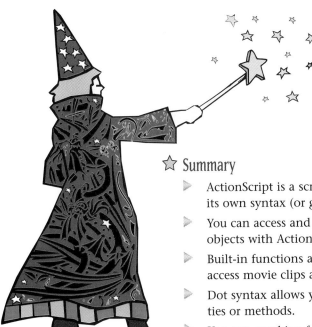

☆ Summary

▷ ActionScript is a scripting or programming language with its own syntax (or grammar), just like any other language.

▷ You can access and manipulate movie clips and other objects with ActionScript.

▷ Built-in functions and properties provide the means to access movie clips and other objects programmatically.

▷ Dot syntax allows you to directly access an object's properties or methods.

▷ You can combine functions and properties with variables, operators, and conditionals. This is where the full power of ActionScript comes from.

▷ You can declare a custom function once and apply it many times throughout a movie.

▷ Good code is more than using the correct syntax. Since an ActionScript rarely works perfectly on the first try, debugging is an essential part of the process.

☆ Online References

Macromedia's ActionScript Support Area and Online Dictionary
`http://www.macromedia.com/support/flash/action_scripts.html`

The Best ActionScript Reference Book
`http://www.moock.org/asdg`

How to Trouble Shoot a Flash Movie
`http://www.macromedia.com/support/flash/ts/documents/troubleshootflash.htm`

Resource Dedicated to Creating Flash ActionScript
`http://www.actionscripts.org/`

Build a Better Preloader
`http://design.oreilly.com/news/action_0501.html`

Using a Menu Smart Clip
`http://www.macromedia.com/support/flash/ts/documents/menu_smartclip.htm`

A Source for Smart Clips
`http://www.flashkit.com/movies/Smart_Clips`

Macromedia Exchange Center, Source for Smart Clips and Components
`http://www.macromedia.com/exchange/flash`

Loading HTML Text into a Flash Movie
`http://www.macromedia.com/support/flash/ts/documents/`
`htmltext.htm`

XML with Flash Example
`http://www.flashkit.com/movies/Scripting/XML/`
`XML_Simp-Jander-2680`

Flash and XML Reference Book
`http://www.FlashandXML.com`

Resources for Building Flash Applications
`http://www.macromedia.com/desdev`

A Few Experimental Web Sites That Use ActionScript
`http://www.yugop.com, http://www.hellodesign.com,`
`http://www.presstube.com, http://www.sodaplay.com`

Flash Games
`http://www.orisinal.com`

Online ActionScript Dictionary
`http://www.macromedia.com/support/flash/action_scripts`

Using JavaScript to Communicate with a Flash Movie
`http://www.macromedia.com/support/flash/publishexport/`
`scriptingwithflash/scriptingwithflash_03.html`

☆ Review Questions

1. What in ActionScript refers to the characteristics of an object that define its transparency, size, and position?

2. Which function, when it works correctly, will display a message in the Output window when tested? What does this function do when you publish a SWF file to the Web?

3. Object-oriented programming doesn't need the *Tell Target* action. What is a more direct way to apply ActionScript?

4. Using the format described in the previous question, how do you apply a method in ActionScript?

5. What part of a movie clip determines where it will align?

6. What is a variable?

7. What type of statement allows you to set requirements for an action?

8. Write two examples of an ActionScript statement that will increase the value of a variable by 4.

9. Why are comments used in a script?

10. Describe two strategies for fixing ActionScript errors.

☆ Hands-On Exercises

1. Refer to Figure 7.3, and write three *setProperty()* functions that will create the transformations that appear in pictures *B*, *C*, and *D*.

2. Add two scripts to two separate buttons. One will change the alpha value of a movie clip to 40%. The second will reposition the same clip to the upper left corner of the Stage.

3. Rewrite this *tellTarget()* script using dot syntax:

```
tellTarget ("bicycleClip/wheel") {
    gotoAndPlay ("animation");
}
```

Use dot syntax to stop the wheel.

4. Create a frame action in a master movie to load another movie. To the master movie also add a button action to move the loaded movie 100 pixels down and 100 pixels to the right, and set its alpha value to 50%. Use *tellTarget()* with slash syntax for this button. Create a second button that uses dot syntax to move the movie to the upper left corner of the Stage and set its alpha value to 100%.

5. Look at the *ifFrameIsLoaded()* function described in Chapter Six. Recreate that functionality using the *_framesloaded* property with an *if* statement in dot syntax.

CHAPTER EIGHT

THE FLASH EXPERIENCE

Y ou've been through it all: from drawing to animation to ActionScript. You should now be familiar with all of the important features of Flash and know how to publish your work on the Web. Now it's time to focus on process. Knowing how to use every last Flash feature doesn't guarantee that every movie you touch will turn golden. How you approach your Flash projects will make the difference between gratuitous noise and compelling content. This chapter focuses on usability (user-friendly design) and other strategies for creating Flash movies that sing. The chapter concludes with suggestions about how to expand your skills in Flash.

Chapter Objectives

☆ Understand when and when not to use Flash

☆ Explain the usability process

☆ Discuss the design flow for a project

☆ Provide a checklist of design practices to follow

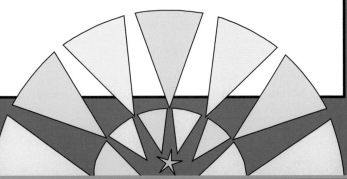

☆ Suggest other topics and tools for creating Flash content

☆ Point the way to improving your Flash skills

◎◉ Consider the Scope of the Project

Know when to use Flash. This implies also knowing when *not* to use Flash. Look at the project before you. If it's for a Web site, don't go in with the preconception that it is a Flash project. Approach it as a Web project, knowing that there may be an opportunity to use Flash.

Does the project warrant the multimedia features that Flash offers? Sometimes it does. If you've got a band and want to promote it with some animation and music samples, Flash may be just the answer. If you are an illustrator, Flash can be a good tool for presenting your work.

On the other hand, the project may work better with just HTML and images. The Cartoon Network site in Figure 8.1 is a perfect venue for Flash, but the Google site is not. When someone goes to a site such as Google.com, they probably are there to search for something, not to be entertained. It can get pretty annoying when someone is looking for a political history of the Czech Republic and they have to wait through a gratuitous animation of bears dancing to techno music. If it's not the right situation for Flash, save those chops for the right project—it will come.

Figure 8.1 The Cartoon Network and Google Web sites.

There's no clear litmus test for when to use Flash and to what extent. Flash may be appropriate, but focused to a single graphic. It may be suitable for one project, but not for another. Many projects fall into a gray area where your judgment and experience come into play. Not only apply what you know, but also seek input from your client and potential users. Here are a few things to consider when starting out on a Flash project.

What Does Flash Offer?

Flash has inherent strengths and weaknesses. Consider them in deciding how Flash fits a project. If there is a compelling advantage to using Flash, many of the weaknesses can be minimized.

Advantages of Flash

☆ Flash is easy to use. When compared to Dynamic HTML and Real Media, it is a relatively easy tool for creating enriched content with sound, interactivity, and animation.

☆ Flash is precise. It offers control over how type and other content is displayed in a pre-defined rectangle. See the "Portable Flash" section at the end of this chapter.

☆ Flash files load fast. If used strategically, Flash provides rich content with a small file size. The download is painless.

☆ Flash is vector-based. This not only saves on file size, but also allows graphic objects to be scaled, distorted, and moved at will.

☆ Flash is rich. Interactivity in Flash can approach the sophistication of a standard software program, such as a game or an address book.

☆ Flash is a standard. It's used on many Web sites today and you probably know other people who already use it to develop Web content. Almost all Web users support some version of the Flash player.

☆ Flash is generally not browser-dependent. Its content displays and behaves consistently between different Web browsers and computer platforms. HTML and JavaScript vary more.

Disadvantages of Flash

☆ Flash movies can be viewed only if the proper plug-in is installed in a Web browser. The vast majority of the Web audience has it, but not everyone does.

☆ Text isn't searchable. Flash's Publish feature adds hidden text to an HTML page to allow basic searching, but it's still not as good as searching for something right on the page. Because of this, Flash loses the edge to HTML for substantial text pages such as news stories.

☆ The newest Flash player has improved access to disabled people, but there's still no way for users to resize the text the way they can with an HTML page. This may appeal to a designer's tendency to control the display of type, but some people who aren't disabled but have poor eyesight may have trouble reading type at the size you choose. Make sure it is legible for everyone, if you want it to be read.

☆ Flash content occupies a distinct rectangle separate from the rest of a Web page. For longer passages of text, you'll have to build a scrolling window within the movie. This means extra work for you and a more complicated interface for your users. Also, there is no reliable way to layer Flash content over other content for all Web browsers.

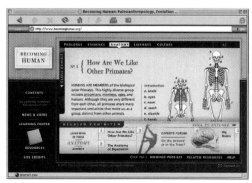 

Figure 8.2 Becominghuman.org is a great Flash multimedia education tool, but don't try the browsers's back button. Also, it's impossible to bookmark a specific section.

 The Web browser's back button can be a real thorn in the design of a Flash site. The back button is one of the most used devices on a Web browser, and users tend to click it often, regardless of any other navigation provided on a page. They may click it while in a Flash movie, expecting to go back to an earlier part of the movie; however, it could take them completely out of the movie, and even to another Web site, with no easy way to return to where they were (see Figure 8.2).

 Bookmarks are problematic. There's no way to bookmark a particular view within a Flash movie for later reference, only the HTML page it is on. In Figure 8.2, the user may think she's saving a bookmark of the view on the left; but when she returns to the bookmark later on, the movie will load the introduction, as demonstrated on the right.

⭐ **TIP**   **Divide a Complex Movie into Separate Web Pages**

If your project is complex and presents several views, divide it into separate movie files and Web pages at logical breaks in the movie. Use the *getURL()* function to link them together (see Chapter Four). This will allow the use of the Web browser's back button and bookmarks. This will also allow other Web pages to link to specific parts within your Flash project.

Flash vs. HTML

Ask yourself how the project could work without Flash. If you can envision the site working just as well or better using HTML and images (and possibly some basic JavaScript), then Flash may not be the answer. If it's a draw between Flash and HTML, stick with HTML because it's simpler and accessible to everyone.

DHTML (Dynamic HTML) combines JavaScript with HTML to do things like create buttons that react visually to the mouse. Some of these techniques are similar to features in Flash, but have the added advantage of being built right into the Web browser itself. With DHTML, you can apply JavaScript to any element on a page, such as text or images, or the Web browser itself. A Flash movie is embedded separately from other content on a Web page and requires a plug-in.

On the other hand, DHTML behaves differently from browser to browser, while Flash is more consistent. DHTML is generally more difficult to implement successfully, especially if you already know how to use Flash. It also is very limited with sound or vector images. Neither strategy is the best for everything.

You have to evaluate each project on its own. If all you want to do is add buttons to a site that respond when the mouse rolls over them, Flash is probably not the best choice. The JavaScript for that behavior is easy to create and works on any browser. The code is widely available for copying from Web development sites such as Webmonkey.com, and it's built in to programs such as Dreamweaver, Fireworks, GoLive, or ImageReady.

If you're looking to add extensive animation and some sound to a page, Flash really is the best for this. And its ActionScript is powerful and easy to implement when compared to DHTML.

> ☆ **TIP**   **Ad Banners in Flash**
>
> Ad banners on Web sites have two requirements: Be as rich as possible and be as small as possible. Flash's vector graphics can provide a fairly involved animation in a small file size. No wonder it's gained a big presence in Web advertising.

How Much Is the Right Amount?

No Web site is 100% Flash. Even if your content is pure Flash, at the least you need an HTML page to embed the movie (see Chapter Six). Few sites successfully tout all Flash-only pages. You could set up the navigation for the entire site with Flash, or you may include some effects to entertain your audience. But when they get to reading that 5-page article, HTML will usually work better.

Is 50% Flash a good proportion? There's no quantifiable amount of Flash that's right. The right amount is when Flash is used appropriately, not gratuitously. Look at the scope of the project. If the goal is to create an illustration, then the answer is simple: either do it in Flash or not. If you are creating a large Web site, then you need to do a lot more analysis and planning to decide where Flash would be appropriate, and you should get the input of others on your team.

◎◉ Design for Your Audience

What good is a Web site if no one can use it? **Usability** is a process of developing something that your audience can actually use. Most of your audience, also referred to as **users**, generally know nothing about Flash. They visit a Web site to read something, to perform a task, or to be entertained. There is only one person who can determine if your project is usable: the user. You need to keep the user in mind throughout the process and consult with potential users to evaluate what you are doing. Think about your users; talk to your users; let your users test your creations. They can teach you a lot.

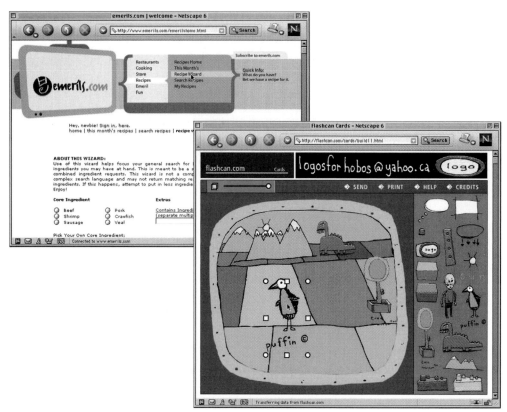

Figure 8.3 Emerils.com uses Flash for the site navigation, but uses HTML for the content. Flashcan.com is a highly interactive site that uses Flash throughout.

Make usability a factor in every project no matter how large or small it is, but scale it to the situation. For an art project or something experimental, it's possible that you may not want the navigation to be obvious. That's fine, but it should be that way for a purpose, not because of neglect.

If you're producing something more practical such as an informational or an e-commerce site, clear navigation is essential. All interactions should give an indication of what the user is doing. Buttons that click with no apparent response, messages that can't be read or comprehended, and anything that leaves a user scratching his head and abandoning the site in dismay should be avoided.

☆ **TIP**   **Usability Can Be Fun**

A usable site does not have to be a dull site. Your approach to a Flash project should integrate creative intuition with design rigor. If you can nourish both sides, your site will flourish. A more playful site can be a more usable site. Boredom would be a real usability problem for an entertainment site, just as a lack of statistics would hurt a financial site.

User-Centered Design

In any Web project, with or without Flash, there are a couple of user-centered design techniques you can apply. Some are more structured and others are just principles to keep in mind.

For a major Web site, the usability process can involve scientific research and controlled user tests. These user tests involve screening potential users, placing them in a controlled environment with a computer, and assigning them specific tasks to test your project.

For a small project, the usability process may involve following usability **heuristics** (design guidelines), getting feedback from colleagues and friends, and running informal user testing. For an informal test, just ask a couple of people to try out your project from their own computers or yours and observe where they get confused or have trouble. For a simple illustration or cartoon, just be cognizant of your audience and show it to a friend or two to get their feedback.

Creating User Profiles and Scenarios

Profiling your audience is a useful exercise for any project. This will help you to visualize how your work would be seen through the eyes of your audience. First, compile demographics that describe your users, such as age, gender, profession, and interests. There will be a range of ages and probably several different types of professions.

Also, compile a list of tasks that they would be trying to accomplish on your site: look up stock quotes, find their way through a cartoon, listen to music. Look at the current site, talk to the client, and interview users to get this information.

From these profiles, write three or four scenarios of different users coming to your site. For example, here are a couple scenarios for a music site:

☆ Gary is 31 and works as a mechanic. He likes to garden and has 3 cats. He also plays guitar for friends on occasion and is coming to the site to find some contemporary music with a Brazilian influence.

☆ Linda is 20 and is a full-time philosophy student who works part time at a convenience store. Right now she sings in a rock band, but her dream is to be an environmental lawyer. Today, she is looking to sample a new song by one of her favorite bands.

These aren't real users, but these scenarios will give life to your design decisions when you can picture actual people using your product.

☆**WARNING** Your Users Don't Know "Flash"

There's a practice on many sites to display a message that gives users a choice between an "HTML Site" and a "Flash Site." The intent is good, but the choices are meaningless to many users. Flash is well known by people building Web sites, but they aren't your only users. It's better not to offer the choice and just build a site that will work well for all of your audience. Otherwise, don't use the word "Flash" (or "HTML"). A more generic phrase such as "Multimedia View" or "Enhanced Mode" would be better received.

Don't Forget the Client

Your client is the person who hired you. It may be your boss at a full-time job or someone who owns a site and hired you for a particular project. Listen to your client for more reasons than just to please her. Your client can also be an ally in the process. She has hired you for a reason. Many business owners invest time and money into market research to understand how to reach a customer base. A customer is a user. The client should already have done a lot of the work in determining the audience and the scope of what you are creating.

Some clients are better prepared than others. If their Web site is selling something, they should know their product and market very well. If they are vague about it, ask them for help defining who their audience is and what the objectives of the Web site are. Ask them for any ideas they may already have concerning the site, and give your feedback if you think you can improve upon their ideas.

Share your ideas and insights too, even if they compete with the client's. Yes, the client does pay you and ultimately has the last word, but she has hired you for your expertise and will usually want to hear what you have to say. In any case, compare your point of view with that of the client; either view by itself will give you an incomplete picture. And don't forget the user.

◎◎ Working in Iterations, A Design Process

Rather than trying to nail down the entire design at once, design in **iterations** (steps). This helps in two ways. First, it frees you from having to get it exactly right on the first try. Second, it gives you room to make changes more easily later on. As a design begins to come to life, you'll notice things that weren't apparent before you started. Also, as you get feedback from colleagues and potential users, you'll want to make revisions.

Sketches and Storyboards

Shut down your computer for the first round of design. This isn't the time to be writing ActionScript or setting up motion tweens. Use pencil and paper, and don't censor yourself (see Figure 8.5). Sketch out a few different ideas, even the stupid ones. Draft a few views of key sections of the movie to demonstrate what changes with interaction. These are called *storyboards*. Make notes on the sketches to indicate potential animation and ActionScript strategies.

Select a couple sketches to show to a trusted friend or colleague. (They may be too crude to show to a client unless you have established a good rapport.) Review your sketches and redo them a second and third time. Even if you think you already have the right design, this may evoke something better. Look at them, refine them, and think about which Flash techniques you might use.

Look over your sketches and decide on the best approach. Discuss this approach and the alternatives with your client and colleagues. You don't necessarily have to show your sketches, unless you have a couple that are more refined. Revise your sketches more, if necessary, until you have a better picture of what you want to start building.

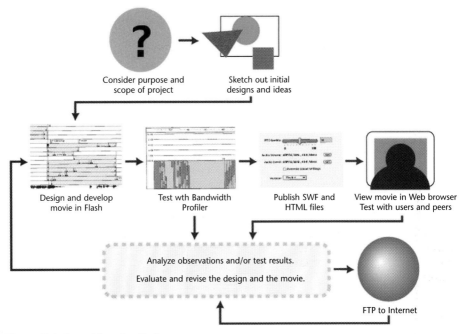

Consider purpose and scope of project

Sketch out initial designs and ideas

Design and develop movie in Flash

Test wth Bandwidth Profiler

Publish SWF and HTML files

View movie in Web browser Test with users and peers

Analyze observations and/or test results.

Evaluate and revise the design and the movie.

FTP to Internet

Figure 8.4 A workflow for Flash.

For simple projects, you can shorten this process, or use a computer drawing program that you are comfortable with. The idea is to start out loose. Once you have developed your sketches and notes, you'll be prepared when you face that blank Flash document.

Build a Prototype

Once you have a better idea of the direction for the project, fire up your computer. It's time to build a prototype or mockup of your project. You still should not be concerned with producing a finished product. Not everything needs to function at this point—this is a refinement of your sketches.

In Flash, build the basic workings first, the infrastructure. If the movie is long, start with one section. Don't worry about getting every interaction and graphic into final form yet. Later on you will come back and refine the artwork, tweak the animations, and complete the actions. This will be the framework for building the final movie.

Seek Feedback from the Client, Users, and Peers

In its half-finished state, share your work with the client and colleagues to get their reactions. You could stage a preliminary test with potential users. Process all the feedback, but don't use it blindly. Take notes first and consider what's relevant later. Make any adjustments that you think are appropriate.

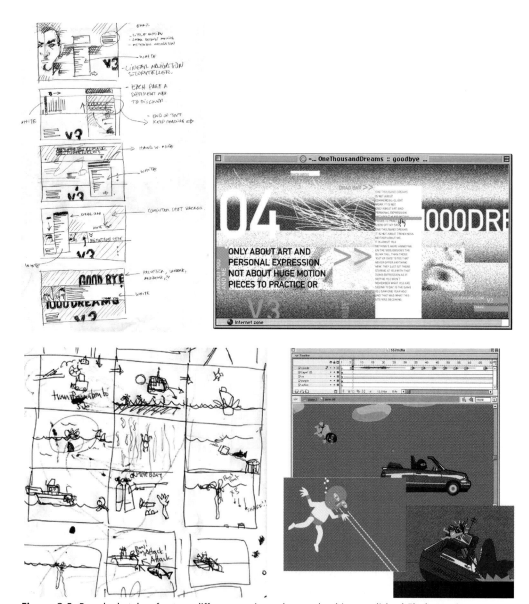

Figure 8.5 Rough sketches for two different projects that evolved into polished Flash movies.

When someone gets lost and doesn't know where to click, that could indicate a weakness. They may even suggest an improvement to the design that you haven't thought of. But if it's a pie-in-the sky request, like, "I want a choice of 100 different soundtracks," you can bring it back to earth.

Refine the Design and the Movie

As the design becomes clearer, refine the movie. Revise the animations, update the artwork, tweak the sounds, and complete the scripts. You'll appreciate symbols at this point. Edit a symbol in the library and all instances on the Stage will be updated (see Figure 6.1). Debug and refine your ActionScripts. Use the Control→Test Movie feature again and again, and revise until it's right. Use the Bandwidth Profiler (explained in Chapter Six) to test your movie and smooth out any bottlenecks.

User Test

As the movie approaches its final form, test it with users again, if possible. Try to use three or four different subjects to compare their feedback. Show them the movie and give them tasks to complete. Observe what they do and take notes. Ask them questions and get their impressions.

Afterward, summarize your notes and evaluate the test. Discuss what worked and didn't work in the test and recommend any changes to the Flash movie. If more than one subject missed a vital button, consider how to help them find it. Show your summary and recommendations to the client and get her feedback, too. Process the feedback and make more adjustments.

☆ SHORTCUT **Quick-and-Dirty User Testing**

Often a project is too small or limited in resources to set up a serious test. In this case, you can test it informally with colleagues or friends. Just set them in front of a computer and give them a few instructions. You could even post the movie at an unadvertised or password-protected Web address and send the address to a few friends along with a list of testing instructions. The important thing is to get someone beside yourself to work with the movie.

Publish the Movie

When the movie has had its final revisions, it's time to publish it. (Chapter Six has more details about this process.) Prepare the HTML page that will hold the final SWF file. View that page locally, on your own computer. Once you are confident that all is working right, it's time to post the HTML and SWF file(s) on your Web site.

Test the Live Movie

Once the content is "live," test it before linking to that page or publicizing it. Try different browsers, computers, and Internet connections, with and without the plug-in. Your testing doesn't need to be this rigorous for a simple, straightforward animation, but if you are using a lot of ActionScript and sound, it should be.

After the movie gets real world use later on, you'll get more feedback. You may want to make additional adjustments to the Flash movie based on what you learn. It's best to avoid errors before posting something live, but this is the Web, so you can make changes to your work at any time.

☆**TIP**   **Pop-Up Flash**

Some sites pop up their Flash content in a separate window (see Figure 8.6). They do this for two reasons. First, it opens a browser window to an ideal size. Also, this can hide the back button and other navigation in the browser window, forcing users to rely solely on the navigation within the Flash content. Sometimes this is a good idea.

   But there are several drawbacks to this technique. Pop-up windows are often mistaken for advertising. When overused, they tend to confuse users and clutter the computer desktop. Try to design without them. For complex projects, break up the Flash into separate movies on separate Web pages. This will allow some navigation from the browser. Design the page so that it looks and works right no matter how someone resizes the browser window.

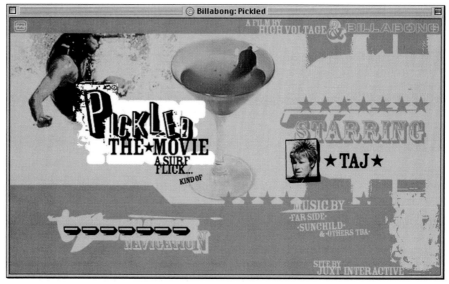

Figure 8.6 Pickledtv.com pops open a browser window without buttons to prevent users from clicking the back button.

◎◎ Good Flash Practices

Flash is a Web medium. Design and usability principles that apply to any Web project apply to Flash. Refer to the *Web Wizard's Guide to Web Design* and the Online References section of this chapter for more about usability design in general. There are a few strategies that you can follow to make Flash specifically more usable (i.e., user-friendly).

☆ Use separate SWF files and unique URLs to divide the Flash content of more complex projects. Use the *getURL()* function to navigate between these sections.

☆ Provide clear navigation. Display links back to your home page and other key points of your Flash project. Users will often want to go back to where they have been and may want to view different sections out of order.

☆ Create an interface that makes sense to your users. They will have an easier time understanding how to use buttons, menus, and other navigational devices if they look familiar. No matter how amazing your work is, your audience spends more time on other Web sites than yours, so it's best to create navigational elements that resemble what they use everyday.

☆ If you expect your users to print information from your Flash movie, learn about the *print()* function, which provides a better way to print content from the movie. (Look on the Web Wizard site for this book for an example of how to do this.) Allow lengthy passages of text to be selectable right in the movie by checking the *Selectable* option in the Text Options panel.

☆ Check to see how the movie will fit in with the rest of the Web page and site. It's one thing to look at a Flash movie by itself, but another to see it in the context of a complete Web page.

☆ Test streaming (from Control→Test Movie) and observe how the movie renders on a computer display.

☆ Use plug-in detection to ensure that the Web page will work with any computer.

☆ Avoid lengthy animated introductions or "splash" pages. If you must use one, be sure to provide a link to skip the introduction.

☆ If possible, avoid popping open a new window with Flash content. If you do use pop-ups, give the user a choice before opening a new window.

☆ Provide an HTML alternative for informational Flash sites.

☆ Give the user control. Allow users to turn off background music. Allow them to bypass anything that's not essential, such as those gratuitous introductions.

☆ FLASH MX   Accessibility Features

Flash MX allows you to designate specific keyframes as **anchors**. This allows the use of the Back button and bookmarks in a Web browser to navigate through a single Flash movie. However, this doesn't work for Macintosh Web browsers or for older Flash plug-ins. Don't rely on this feature for a mass audience, but it can't hurt if you want to apply it for those who do support it.

The new **Accessibility** panel in Flash MX goes far to address the concerns of providing content for disabled users. With it, you can label objects in your Flash movie so that blind users with screen readers can easily navigate through your movie and comprehend its content better. See the Flash MX manual for more about these features.

◎◎ Beyond Flash

You will build on the techniques covered in this book as you gain more experience with Flash. If you want, you can extend Flash beyond those boundaries by combining it with other software products. This section describes a few ways to branch out with Flash.

Portable Flash

Flash is not just for the personal computer. Flash may be everywhere one day, even in your kitchen appliances. It's probably the most convenient tool for creating specialized Web-based interfaces in a confined area. This is an emerging application of Flash, but already you can use it to design content for hand-held computers that use Pocket PC software. See the Online References section at the end of this chapter for links to more information.

Web-Based Applications

With ActionScript, you can coax Flash to do some pretty amazing things. Add the power of a Web server, and you can create full-feature Web-based applications. This includes e-mail services, online organizers, interactive shopping carts, reservations systems, chat utilities, and more; all with the multimedia features of Flash.

Flash works great on its own. All you need to do is copy a SWF file to any Web server to make Flash live. A few years ago, Flash Generator was released as a Web server application that's just for Flash. It uses specialized templates that you create in Flash. The templates allow you to connect Flash content to a database and customize it for each user. It even works with Flash 3-compatible content. However, Flash Generator is no longer supported in Flash MX.

The XML support introduced in Flash 5 has even more capabilities that don't require Flash Generator. In place of it, you can use Macromedia Cold Fusion or other popular server technologies to create anything in Flash that you could with HTML, and even more. One day, we may be doing all of our banking and shopping through Flash, or using it to play the latest video games, all via the Internet.

Using Flash with QuickTime

When you are displaying video footage on the Web, Apple's QuickTime is the preferred format. It can also import Flash files allowing you to combine the buttons, interactivity, and other features of Flash within a QuickTime movie. Likewise, Flash 5 can import QuickTime movies, but you must export your work in the QuickTime format (not SWF) to take advantage of it. See the Flash reference for more about this.

☆ **FLASH MX   QuickTime Support**

Flash MX supports embedded video content within a Flash movie. A Flash MX file with QuickTime content can be exported faithfully in the SWF format. Also, you can apply transformations, effects, and actions to a QuickTime movie as you would to other objects.

Beyond Flash

Adobe LiveMotion

Naturally, Flash is the standard for creating Flash content, but there are other tools. Adobe's LiveMotion creates the same SWF files that Flash does, but it has a completely different Timeline for animation that some people prefer; it resembles Adobe After Effects. If you are interested mostly in creating animations and basic interactivity, it may be worth a try.

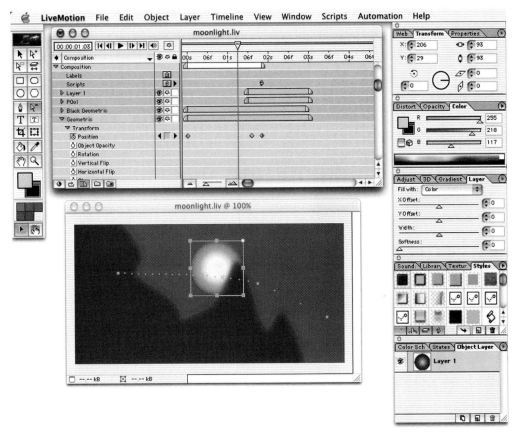

Figure 8.7 Adobe LiveMotion Timeline.

Version 2 of LiveMotion catches up to Flash 5's scripting capabilities. It also works directly with Photoshop and Illustrator files and integrates well into GoLive. If you use all of these Adobe programs a lot, you should give LiveMotion a try.

On the downside, you cannot share work files between LiveMotion and Flash, so if you collaborate on projects, you and your colleagues will all need to use the same program. Also, LiveMotion is behind Flash in some key features, most notably in its lack of a symbol library. It also lags in the latest ActionScript capabilities in Flash MX. (However, the LiveMotion scripting capabilities may be adequate for you.)

Other SWF-Building Programs

Flash doesn't support 3D animation. You can use Swift 3D to create a single 3D object, or apply its robust animation, texture, and lighting features to move and turn objects through space (see Figure 8.8). When you are done, Swift 3D can export a SWF file for use in Flash.

☆**WARNING No Native 3D in Flash**

Flash doesn't have the ability to turn objects in three-dimensional space. Programs such as Swift 3D emulate the dimensional effect with a series of frame-by-frame drawings, which is much less efficient than tweening symbols. This is all right if you use it in moderation and find no performance problem, but using 3D animation throughout a long movie can create very large SWF files.

Another program, 3D Flash Animator also creates 3D artwork. Other programs such as SWiSH and KoolMoves apply special effects to Flash content. All of these programs save SWF files that you can import to use in a Flash work file.

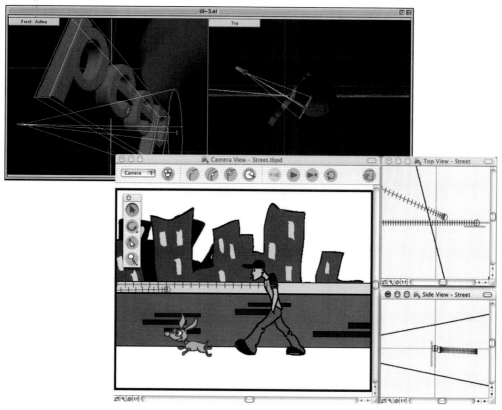

Figure 8.8   Swift 3D (top). Toon Boom Studio (bottom).

Beyond Flash

If you want to create character animation or Flash cartoons, you should consider using Toon Boom Studio (see Figure 8.8). Its tools work like a movie set to help you move cartoon characters through three-dimensional space, while working the camera angle. Toon Boom Studio exports SWF files, complete with symbols and sounds that you can import into Flash 5. Flash MX seamlessly imports native Toon Boom files with its layers intact for an easier workflow.

◎◉ The Road to Flash Mastery

This book is your foundation to learning the Flash program. There's a lot more ahead of you as you put your knowledge to use. Here are a few tips for expanding your Flash skills. Keep these in mind and you'll continue to improve:

- ☆ **Practice makes perfect.** Just start using it. That's the best way to become a master.
- ☆ **Collaborate with others.** Share what you learn and listen to what your friends and colleagues have learned.
- ☆ **Join online communities.** There's a good mailing list in the Online References section of Chapter One, and you'll come across others. Learn from experts and get to know others who are working on similar problems.
- ☆ **Consult resources.** Use the Online References at the end of each chapter in this book and the accompanying Web sites. There's a wealth of information online and in print on every intricacy of Flash.
- ☆ **Use good practices.** As you apply usability and create more appropriate content, these practices will become second nature.
- ☆ **Never be afraid to try something new.** Trying out a new technique may frustrate you at first, but it will quickly become familiar.
- ☆ **Do some planning, but not too much.** Sketch out your ideas on paper, and revise them as the project progresses. Don't be afraid to change course later on.

☆ **SHORTCUT Keep Looking Around**

Look at as many Web sites as possible. Share addresses with Flash friends, and use the links in this book. Look at sites with a critical eye, taking note of what works and what doesn't, and why. Discuss this with your friends and colleagues. Like other Flash skills, good design requires practice. Learn from others so you don't have to make every mistake yourself, and learn it all from scratch.

The Road to Flash Mastery

☆ Summary

▷ To use Flash properly, you also need to know when *not* to use it, and how much to use it.

▷ Usability is more than following a specific set of guidelines; it's a process. Throughout the development of a project, pay attention to the way users interact with the movie and listen to the comments of colleagues and clients.

▷ Design iteratively, refining and revising all the way until the project is published.

▷ There are several other programs that expand the way you can create Flash content.

☆ Online References

Jakob Nielsen's Principles for Usability
`http://www.useit.com/papers/heuristic`

Flash Usability Information
`http://www.flazoom.com/usability`

Making Flash Accessible for Everyone
`http://www.macromedia.com/software/flash/productinfo/accessibility`

Macromedia Flash Usability Resources
`http://www.macromedia.com/software/flash/productinfo/usability`

Using Flash with QuickTime
`http://www.macromedia.com/software/flash/qt4`

Create Flash Screen Savers
`http://www.screentime.com/ScreenTime/screentime.html`

Flash for Pocket PCs
`http://www.pocketpcflash.net`

Site Dedicated to 3-D Flash
`http://www.popedeflash.com`

Swift 3D
`http://www.swift3d.com`

3D Flash Animator
`http://www.insanetools.com`

KoolMoves
`http://www.koolmoves.com`

SWiSH
`http://www.swishzone.com`

Adobe LiveMotion
`http://www.adobe.com/products/livemotion`

Toon Boom Studio
`http://www.toonboomstudio.com`

☆ Review Questions

1. How much Flash should you use for a single project?

2. List two weaknesses and two strengths of Flash.

3. Who is the expert in determining how usable a Web site is?

4. Describe two practices for making Flash more usable.

5. Is Flash a good choice for a music or entertainment site? Why or why not?

6. In general, what is the best tool for a serious news Web site: Flash or HTML? Explain your answer.

7. Who probably best knows the audience for an existing Web site?

8. At which part of the process should you consider the audience for a project?

9. What tools do you use at the very beginning of the design process for a Flash movie?

10. Is a Web project's design ever final? Explain your answer.

☆ Hands-On Exercises

1. Go to the Web and browse the following sites.

   `http://www.yahoo.com`
   `http://www.ew.com`
   `http://udel.edu/~mm/anime/speed`
   `http://www.travelocity.com`

   Which ones would be the best candidates for using Flash? Why? Pick one and describe what the scope of Flash would be (from a single illustration to the entire site). Describe a few ideas and include rough sketches.

2. You are designing a short Flash cartoon. Make a storyboard to describe the cartoon.

3. Invent a fictitious idea for a new Web site. Describe the objectives of the site and its intended audience. Create three user profiles based on this.

4. Look at the homepage for `http://www.weather.com/maps`. Draw up a list of three or four tasks you want tested on that page. Ask a classmate or friend to pose as your test subject. Ask them to complete your list of tasks

and take notes on what you observe. Summarize what you learned from this exercise and what changes you would make to the page.

5. Using Flash, create a mockup with a new design for the page you tested in Exercise 4. The mockup will be visual—it doesn't have to work. (Don't include the advertising at the top of the existing page or the links at the bottom.) Make changes to it based on your test experience and observations.

APPENDIX: ANSWERS TO ODD-NUMBERED REVIEW QUESTIONS

Chapter One

1. A bitmap image uses many pixels or tiny squares to compose a complete image. A vector image uses geometry to describe the shapes and colors of objects. Flash emphasizes vector images.

3. A work file or work document is where you do your work in Flash. Flash work files conventionally end with the .fla file extension suffix (e.g., *myfile.fla*). From a work file, Flash publishes SWF files for viewing on a Web page. These files must have the .swf file extension suffix to play in a Web browser (*myfile.swf*).

5. In Flash you create artwork and edit it on the Stage. The Stage determines what is displayed in a Flash movie.

7. Layers are an organizational tool for separating elements and juxtaposing them one in front of another.

9. You can open any panel from the Windows menu. In Flash 5, many of them are available under the Panels submenu. *Flip Horizontal* is available from the Transform submenu, which is part of the Modify menu.

Chapter Two

1. Frame rate and other settings that affect the entire Flash movie are available from the Movie Properties window (Modify→Movie). For Flash MX, it's called Document Properties and you can access these settings from the Properties Inspector by clicking on an empty area of the Stage.

3. Draw with the Paint Brush tool to create fill shapes without strokes. If you want to add a stroke to a fill shape, click on it with the Ink Bottle tool.

5. The Arrow tool is the most popular tool in Flash. Use it to select, modify, or move objects on the Flash stage. To remove a selected object, press the Del key on the keyboard.

7. The Swatches, Mixer, and Tool panels allow you to change colors for any tool or selection. In Flash 5 there's also the Stroke and Fill panels. In Flash MX, the Properties Inspector allows you to change the stroke or fill of any selection.

9. Select a text block with the Arrow tool and apply Modify→Break Apart to break it into a standard vector object. In Flash MX, you'll have to repeat this command a second time.

◎◎ Chapter Three

1. Keyframes denote change in the Timeline and usually correspond to a change on the Stage as well.

3. A motion tween uses only two keyframes, but creates an animation that runs for several frames.

5. Place a symbol instance on the Stage. Every instance refers to an original symbol in the library.

7. Use the Tint effect to change the color of a symbol instance.

9. Click the Edit Multiple Frames button at the bottom of the Timeline and you can select and edit objects in more than one frame. Open the Onion Markers that surround the playhead to include every frame in the movie. Make sure that all of your layers are unlocked and choose Edit→Select All to select everything in the movie. Once selected, you can reposition everything at once.

◎◎ Chapter Four

1. In Flash, there are movie events and user events. Movie events are generally triggered by a keyframe in the Timeline and user events are often triggered by buttons.

3. Use the *Stop* action to stop the play of a movie and the *Play* action to start it again.

5. The *Go To* action allows a movie to jump straight to any frame.

7. You can save parts of your Flash project into separate SWF files. From the main movie use the *Load Movie* action to seamlessly load the separate SWF files into it.

9. Once you name a movie clip instance, it can be the target of a *Tell Target* action. *Tell Target* allows an action to target any named movie clip in a Flash movie.

◎◎ Chapter Five

1. Like other assets, sounds are stored in a movie's library. From there, you can specify an individual sound's compression settings.

3. Sounds are applied to keyframes on the Timeline. With a keyframe selected, use the Sound panel in Flash 5 or the Properties Inspector in Flash MX.

5. The *StopAllSounds* action will stop any sound from playing. Apply a specific sound with the stop sync to stop just that sound from playing.

7. To maximize sound compression, you must balance sound quality with file size. Better quality adds to the file size, but overcompress a sound and its quality will suffer.

9. MP3 compression works well for general sounds and sound loops, but ADPCM compression can get you better quality and compression for short sound effects.

◎◎ Chapter Six

1. Bandwidth is the amount of information that can transmit through a network over a period of time. Reducing the size of a Flash file reduces the amount of information to be transmitted, thus improving bandwidth.

3. Flash utilizes built-in streaming so that one part of a movie can be viewed as other content for later viewing loads in the background.

5. Use the Movie Explorer to find symbol instances, actions, and text in a movie.

7. The Flash tab from File→Publish Settings allows you to change the default sound compression and other settings for a published SWF file.

9. The best way to test a movie is to closely mimic the conditions that your audience will experience when viewing it. Use a Web browser that loads the HTML and Flash content in the same way as it would for your users.

◎◎ Chapter Seven

1. In ActionScript, a movie clip object has properties that define its transparency, size, and position.

3. ActionScript is an object-oriented language that uses dot syntax to target objects and apply actions to them.

5. The registration point determines where a movie aligns. The Info panel positions an object based on it.

7. A conditional statement allows you to set requirements for an action. The *if* statement is the most popular type of conditional.

9. Comments are used in scripts to hide lines of code and to add notes that document code.

◎◎ Chapter Eight

1. There is no definite amount of Flash that will work for every project. You must weigh the objectives of each project to determine what media are appropriate. If you are using Flash, you will decide whether it's for a single graphic, the entire site, or something in between.

3. Only the user really knows what works for the himself or herself. Listen to your users and keep them in mind throughout the design and development process of a Web project.

5. For a purely entertainment site, such as a game or a music sampler, Flash could be just the thing for most of the site. Its animation and sound features would be well received by the audience. If the site is a more general entertainment site with news and articles to read, then you may want to hold back on using Flash, except for an occasional feature.

7. Your client should have a good idea of the goals of a project and who the audience is for a Web site. Ask your client who the audience is and if this information isn't available, ask your client to help you find it out.

9. Pencil and paper is the best technology when starting a Flash project. If you are more natural with a drawing program such as Adobe Illustrator, then you can start with that instead.

INDEX

CREDITS

Figure 1.1a	Screenshot courtesy of NCSA and The University of Illinois.
Figure 1.1b, 8.6	Juxt Interactive
Figure 1.3b	Katbot, its characters, elements & indicia, and Funny Garbage all © and ™ Funny Garbage Inc.
Figures 1.5, 3.2, 3.5, 3.9, 3.10, 4.8, 6.1, 7.5, 8.4	Illustrations by Gary Bernal (gb@peep.org)
Figures 3.4, 3.7, 3.13, 6.4	Illustrations by Jonathan Louie (jonathan@sinuous.com)
Figure 6.2	Courtesy of AnimationExpress.com and artist, Steve Whitehouse, www.whitehouseanimationinc.com
Figure 6.5a	Courtesy of AnimationExpress.com and artist, Chad Essley.
Figure 6.8, 8.3	Netscape Communicator browser window© 1999 Netscape Communications Corporation. Used with permission. Netscape Communications has not authorized, sponsored, endorsed, or approved this publication and is not responsible for its content.
Figure 8.1a	™ and © Cartoon Network and/or Hanna-Barbera. An AOL Time Warner Company. All Rights Reserved. LOONEY TUNES, characters, names and all related indicia are trademarks and © Warner Bros 2002. BATMAN, WONDER WOMAN and all related characters and elements are trademarks of DC Comics © 2002.
Figure 8.1b	Google, Inc.
Figure 8.2	BecomingHuman.org. Used with permission.
Figure 8.3a	The EMERILS.COM logo is the trademarked property of Food of Love Productions, LLC. EMERILS.COM is the official web site of Chef Emeril Lagasse.
Figure 8.3b	Courtesy of zinc Roe design and Craig Marshall.
Figure 8.5b	Naoki Mitsuse, www.goultralightsgo.com
Figure 8.7	Adobe and LiveMotion are either registered trademarks of Adobe Systems Incorporated in the United States and/or other countries.
Figure 8.8b	Toon Boom Studio®